Write to Read

Ready-to-use classroom lessons that
explore the ABCs of writing

Larry Swartz

Pembroke Publishers Limited

Dedication
To Jennifer Rowsell, dear friend

Acknowledgment

Thanks to David Booth, mentor and friend, especially for his books *The ABC's of Creative Writing* and *The Writing Program* (Globe Modern Curriculum Press), which planted seeds and inspiration for *Write to Read*.

© **2022 Pembroke Publishers**
538 Hood Road
Markham, Ontario, Canada L3R 3K9
www.pembrokepublishers.com

Library and Archives Canada Cataloguing in Publication

Title: Write to read : easy-to-use classroom lessons that explore the ABCs of writing / Larry Swartz.

Names: Swartz, Larry, author.

Description: Includes bibliographical references and index.

Identifiers: Canadiana (print) 20220416427 | Canadiana (ebook) 20220416451 | ISBN 9781551383590 (softcover) | ISBN 9781551389608 (PDF)

Subjects: LCSH: Language arts (Elementary) | LCSH: Writing—Study and teaching (Elementary) | LCSH: Reading (Elementary)

Classification: LCC LB1576 .S93 2022 | DDC 372.62/3—dc23

Editor: Kat Mototsune
Cover Design: John Zehethofer
Typesetting: Jay Tee Graphics Ltd.

Printed and bound in Canada
9 8 7 6 5 4 3 2 1

Contents

Preface

> "Let us remember: One book, one pen, one child and one teacher can change the world."
> —Malala Yousafzai, activist, author

As I embark on writing this preface, I dig into my own elementary education. Sadly, I can't remember a single thing I wrote from Grades 1 to 6. I can say that any writing done in the classroom was in response to assigned tasks, without much choice offered. I do remember book reports following a rigid template to respond to novels read independently in Grades 7, 8, and 9. I remember writing reports in preparation for giving speeches in front of the class: Color Blindness (Grade 7); The Invention of Television (Grade 8); All About Blood (Grade 8). (Thank you, Dad, for buying a set of encyclopedia for the family.) I remember writing an essay in high school called "A is for Apples" (for which I got an A).

To be frank, putting together an effective writing program always posed a challenge for me as a literacy teacher, year by year, from primary to intermediate grades. In my beginning years as a teacher, I remember assigning topics and collecting student writing (often on foolscap), circling errors in spelling and grammar. The Halloween mystery story, a poem about peace, story starters, the answers to questions about literature—these all seemed to be the stuff of my students' writing. But there were two meaningful road bumps on my journey as a writing teacher. For the first, I took continuing education courses in Literacy and met David Booth, Jo Phenix, and Ron Benson, who lit a match that initiated change. I sought ways to better consider writing across the curriculum. I recognized a need to introduce a variety of genres and provide students with examples and instruction that would develop their skills. Then I met Lucy Calkins, Shelley Harwayne, Donald Graves, and Regie Routman through their books (and, yes, through workshops), and their writing changed my teaching to better consider the process and authentic writing possibilities. As I worked towards doing better, several books motivated me to revisit and refine my practice: *In the Middle* by Nancy Atwell, *Reading and Writing in the Middle Years* by David Booth, *Craft Lessons* and *Non-Fiction Craft Lessons* by Ralph Fletcher, *I Am a Pencil* by Sam Swope, and Lucy Calkins' *Living Between the Lines*.

The experience of writing a thesis helped me to dig even deeper into the connection between reading and writing as I researched the role of reading response journals. When students are asked to write about their reading, they are being encouraged to reflect on what a book has meant to them and how they made meaning of the text. Written responses, whether they are derived from teacher questions or prompts, or are recorded independent of instructions, invite students to present ideas in a variety of genres. Moreover, the thoughts, questions, and connections students reveal can be—should be—shared with others, and in this way the classroom further becomes a community of readers and writers.

As a university instructor teaching Literacy for teacher candidates working in elementary classrooms, I have 12 weeks to provide information, raise awareness, and inform teachers of best literacy practices that help them meet curriculum expectations. My classes in writing are perhaps limited to only two sessions, one of which is devoted to analyzing student samples to consider the wide range of contexts in which students write, how to provide feedback, and how to assess writing. In a three-hour class I tell students about my journey, I provide samples of student notebooks, I have the students participate in a quickwrite experience, we investigate webinars and YouTube videos available to further inform them. I share mentor texts to let candidates know children's literature and professional resources to guide and support them. Thirty-six hours to teach the spectrum of literacy programs when, in fact, the entire course could be about writing. Upon completion of my university literacy courses, I ask students what questions remain about teaching writing, Overwhelmingly, the answer is *Motivation, Motivation, Motivation*. How do you inspire students to write? How can we introduce the range of writing genres to our students? How can we meet the diverse needs of students, some who may be hesitant to write, others who are proficient writers?

I am a reminded of a professional development session I was invited to many years ago, to facilitate for a group of teachers of Grades 1 to 9. Note: This workshop took place several years before there were computers or tablets in the classrooms, before the words *email*, *texting*, and *smart* were part of every day lingo. The topic of my session was *Reading and Writing: What's the Connection?* I began the workshop by inviting participants to list the writing they had done within the past week: a grocery list, a thank-you note, report card comments, a note to a student, a to-do list, a letter to a friend, a journal entry, instructions for a science experiment, a message of condolence, an announcement for a bake sale, etc. The word *story* or *poem* did not appear on anyone's list. What do such lists tell us about the writing tasks we present in our classrooms? What is the balance of fiction and nonfiction writing we offer? How do we prepare students to experience authentic writing they might do outside of class and into their future lives in the workplace? How do the students see themselves as writers outside of a designated time in the literacy block? How can we offer students a range of different writing modes, with different purposes, for different audiences?

Write to Read is written to provide both beginning and experienced teachers with a carousel of writing lessons to use to plan and develop programs where all students can feel successful as they put pencil or pen to paper, finger to keyboard. It is a collection of best practices I have used in my own classroom, witnessed as a guest in the classrooms of others, demonstrated in my university literacy classes with beginning teachers, and shared in extensive professional development workshops locally and afar. This resource offers a grab bag of diverse classroom-tested activities to address the diverse interests and skills of students.

Each lesson presented in *Write to Read* is directed to the student and includes:

- a description of the writing mode
- a Read to Write component that provides suggestions of anchor texts of fiction, nonfiction, or poetry selections to set the context and inspire students to Write to Read
- a Write to Read strategy with step-by-step instructions
- a Let's Go Further component to motivate students to practice and apply their understanding of a writing mode in alternative contexts.

Reproducible masters are included to support and guide a number of writing modes, and for you to use as you help students explore their lives as writers. By offering the students these masters, you are offering them prompts and suggestions to motivate them to write in such modes as journals, recounts, memoirs, questioning, quickwrites, and reading response journals.

"When a writing assignment demands interaction with the reader, an adult or a peer, it is more likely that students will work hard to make it their best. …Students need to see that their words can make a reader smile, sigh, nod, laugh or even tear up."
—Shelley Harwayne (2021, page 5)

Use the Thinking About My Writing reproducible on page 116 to help students learn more about who they are as writers.

Introduction

> "Writing is a complex act, a symbolic system—a means of representing thought, concepts and feelings—that involves memory and ordering of symbols to communicate ideas and feelings to others."
> —David Booth, *Literacy Techniques*

> "Writers 'gift' their readers with words in the hope of touching them in some way—through laughter or tears, questions, connections, visual images. Writers share pieces of themselves and the things they care about with their readers, reaching out to them with an unspoken invitation to think."
> —Adrienne Gear, *Writing Power*

Talk is thought out loud. Writing is putting thought on paper (or screen), and learning to communicate through writing is a cumulative, lifelong process. No matter the curriculum subject, the topic, or the reason for writing, it is important that teachers explain how each function of writing works in each genre, from recounts, to letters, to journals, to reflecting on our reading. It is important that students know the purpose/function of their writing activities and who the audience for their writing will be. Reading and writing are closely connected processes of learning. A student writing down their thoughts thinks and reads while composing, revising, rereading, and editing the final product. Sometimes the audience for the writing is the self. Moreover, writing, as a form of communication, needs to be read by others. Students need to write to be read.

Our literacy programs need to provide explicit instruction in the writer's craft particular to each genre/mode/form. Mini-lessons, demonstrations, and mini-conferences are essential to the development of students' writing. Reading a genre should support student genre writing. Mentor texts can provide students with useful models of writing that provide patterns and suggestions on how to arrange thoughts and information. Students need to read to write.

The traditional motivation of writing in the classroom has not been a student's inner compulsion to write, but the completion of assigned writing tasks. It is important that today's writing curricula stress the uses of writing and lead students to understand that they are writing for real purposes. When writers write in a context that has personal significance, they reach for the necessary skills to explore both content and form. As students begin to think of themselves as writers, they discover that they can control what they want to say to the people they want to reach presented in *Write to Read*.

With social media, students in the 21st century are writing more than they ever have. Sending an email or a text is part of our everyday lives that likely doesn't require motivation or direction. However, our classroom writing programs can be, should be, a place where students are taught about the sea of writing possibilities. Student writing can be one of any number of modes—personal, narrative, anecdotal, research-related, fantastical, questioning, in-role, opinion-ated, explanatory, etc.

The words of two popular children's authors can serve as a stepping stone for this resource as teachers and their students work together to write more, write better, write with purpose.

"Writing is like any sort of sport. In order for you to get better at it, you have to exercise the muscle."
—Jason Reynolds

"Do not sit there like, 'Oh I don't feel like it today. I don't feel like it tomorrow.' Feel like it! Do it! Force yourself!"
—James Patterson

Read to Write

Reading and writing are learned hand in hand, the one enriching the other. We can reinforce the reading-writing connection in two ways:

1. Using children's literature as mentor texts
2. Providing time and strategies for students to write about their reading

Mentor Texts

"The 'fingerprints' of the authors' craft found in mentor texts often become our own. ... They ignite the writer's imagination and determination to create high quality text that mirrors the mentor text in many ways."
—Lynn Dorfman & Rose Cappelli (2009, page 7)

To help young writers learn how to do what they may not yet be able to do on their own, we can turn to mentor texts. When students borrow from their reading as they write, they are writing as readers and reading like writers. We cannot teach writing without providing the best possible examples of how it is done. Picture books, novels, poetry, and nonfiction texts provide inspiration, spring-boards, and authentic demonstrations of the craft of writing. Students who learn to read with real books see how writers represent experience. Whether listening to a book being read aloud or reading a book independently, students can learn

- to borrow ideas, structure, and vocabulary for their own writing
- about the craft of writing, (e.g., word choice, style, description, transcription)
- how text features work (e.g., headings, captions, lists, speech balloons)
- how to describe characters and places, and how to emphasize what is significant in a plot for narrative writing.
- how to present factual information and inform readers of important ideas

Written Responses to Reading

When readers are asked to write about their reading, they are being encouraged to reflect on what a book has meant to them and how they made meaning of the text. Written responses, whether derived from teacher questions/prompts or independent of instructions, invite students to present ideas in a variety of genres. Moreover, the thoughts, questions, and connections students reveal can be, and should be, shared with others to read and to discuss, thus helping students consider the thoughts of others, which may or may not be similar to their own. In this way, the classroom further becomes a community of readers and writers.

Write to Read

All writing is meant to be read, if only by the writer. The audience for a piece of writing depends on its function and the reasons for sharing it. Journals, notes, and first drafts, for example, are often private and personal. Students may decide to discuss some pieces with a trusted adult (a teacher, a volunteer, a parent) who will respond to the content in an interested and supportive way. Other pieces will be read by peers—at a draft stage, in a group conference, in a collaborative activity, or as published or displayed finished work. Emails and text messages have given authentic purpose for writing to be read. Students may also write for unknown audiences (e.g., a persuasive letter, a school newsletter, a classroom blog, or for passers-by who glance at a bulletin board). Each context can provide young authors with a sense of the various functions, styles, and conventions of writing, and of the importance of accuracy and neatness.

Authentic audiences include

- Self (diary, lists, reading responses)
- Friends (emails, questions)
- Classmates (essays, narratives, poetry, brochures, autobiographies)
- Parents (newsletters, published works)
- Teachers (reports, response journals)
- Known and unknown audiences (reviews, announcements)

Adapted from *Reading and Writing in the Middle Years* by David Booth

Writing Goals for Students

1. Write each day for a variety of purposes.
2. Keep a writer's notebook in order to gather and collect observations and ideas for future writing projects.
3. Record feelings and experiences.
4. Choose most topics for your writing projects.
5. Write in a variety of genres.
6. Use different formats for different projects.
7. Learn about the craft of writing from noticing how authors work.
8. Participate in conferences with the teacher and other students.
9. Share your writing with classmates, and listen to and read theirs.
10. Request feedback from others in planning and revising your writing.
11. Revisit writing to revise and edit original drafts.
12. Integrate reading, talk, and writing.
13. Understand and apply success criteria to complete writing projects.
14. See yourself as a writer in all areas of the curriculum.
15. Use digital tools effectively in writing projects.
16. Publish a writing project each month.

Ten Essentials for Writing to Read

Choice Matters

How much choice do students have in their writing topics? Does the notebook or reading response journal give students freedom to write in different forms and record personal responses? Do writing prompts serve to motivate student writing? Do mentor texts inspire students to write? Are students inspired by the writing of their friends? How much choice do students have in the way they

The Thought Starters list on page 117 provides students with prompts for writing. Students can choose items from the list to motivate their writing in a variety of genres. Alternately, you can choose and post items from this list for students to focus on.

Resources that can effectively serve teachers in the use of mentor texts in their writing programs:
Mentor Texts by Lynn R. Dorfman and Rose Cappelli (also: *Nonfiction Mentor Texts*)
Powerful Writing Structures by Adrienne Gear.

present their writing, share their writing, publish their writing? Is there a balance between assigned writing tasks and student choices? In this book, teachers are given the opportunity to introduce a format or pattern for students to practice. Still, throughout the resource, suggestions are provided that invite students to make choices about the topics, prompts, and content that they choose to use, while still meeting the success criteria for each format.

Mentor Texts Matter

Mentor texts help develop relationships with authors and their work. If you want students to write effective lead sentences, it's important to provide them with examples from literature as models. If you want students to write memoirs, mystery stories, or myths, share examples of how published authors have done this effectively. One of most meaningful ways to teach students about different writing genres or writing formats is to provide literature and, through writer's workshop, explain and analyze how the author has been successful at engaging readers. Mentor texts (aka Anchor Texts) are written pieces, whether found in a book, magazine, or teacher and/or student writing, that can serve as an example of good writing for student writers. The texts are read for the purpose of studying the author's craft, or the way the author uses words and structures in the writing. The goal is to provide students with a model they could emulate in crafting their own written work. Moreover, when we use mentor texts in our classrooms, we teach students to read like writers.

Talk Matters

In a writing block of thirty minutes, how much time do students actually spend putting pencil to paper, or finger to keyboard? To prepare for writing with any given task, many students need time to talk to percolate ideas. For many students, opportunities to talk prepare and motivate them in their writing. For example, when writing a recount, the oral retelling of events is a rehearsal for what students will put into writing. For expository writing, students might turn to a partner to explain instructions and this conversation helps them with sequencing and the need for presenting ideas with clarity. *Let Talk Precede Writing* is a good rule to implement in the writing program.

Talk, however, shouldn't be limited to before-writing experiences. Some students need to chat with others to help them clarify ideas, receive advice, request information (including spelling and grammar). The oral feedback that students receive from their classmates as they write can be supportive and motivating. And when students share their completed writing projects with others, they invite feedback and suggestions from an audience, thus determining how successful they were at keeping the reader in mind for their written work.

Feedback Matters

When assessing student work, avoid simple judgments, such as "That's interesting!" or "I liked your story." It is important to look for a piece's strengths and perhaps weaknesses and to consciously provide constructive advice that relates directly to the student's written work. When receiving feedback, whether written or in a writing conference, a student feels their knowledge of the writers' craft is acknowledged. Also, less is more. Feedback should be focused, be explicit, and offer examples or specific suggestions for improvement.

"The writing workshop is a gathering place of passionate ideas and opinions. It is the room where our students can go to imagine and reimagine the world."
—Kwame Alexander (2019)

See Revision Checklist on page 118.

Writing with Others Matters

Most often, students are given the opportunity and choice to write independently. However, some writing formats are more conducive to the collaborative experience (e.g., group reports, brainstorming, brochures, transcription). As students plan, develop, and present written work with a partner or small group, they can share ideas, negotiate ideas, and hitchhike off one another's thoughts. Having students work together, blending skills, talents, and interests, helps to promote communication and build a writing community.

Revising and Editing Matter

Revising and editing are two different processes. Students need to become aware that what most interests readers about their writing is what they have to say, not just their typos and errors. Editing is about correcting errors in grammar and spelling. Revision deals with the flow of narrative or ideas, relevance of information, and clarity of expression. Teachers tend to spend too much time focusing on editing, but by providing feedback suggesting changes, by providing explicit instruction on the craft of writing through one-on-one, small-group, or whole-class demonstrations, teachers can help students to revisit and refine their work.

Teachers need to engage students in their writing so that they will want to continue the writing process, which means students rethink and revisit their writing to develop strength or clarity, to alter its organization, or to select effective words and language structure. Not every piece of writing will be edited and revised. Many pieces benefit from being left unattended, even for a day or two. A fresh reading often can highlight changes that need to be made. Sharing a published piece by each student in the classroom at various points in the year (once a month?) is a positive reinforcement for their work.

Audience Matters

Students may be motivated to refine and polish their writing when they are preparing for an authentic audience. Yes, the teacher should be considered an important audience, but not the only one. Do students have opportunities to share their work with classmates, with a writing buddy or editing group, with others in the school, with families, with others in the community, with anonymous readers? A classroom blog or website is a meaningful tool for students to share their writing in a variety of capacities (e.g., newsletters, reports, collaborative books, persuasive letters). It is also worth noting that writers themselves are significant audiences; some writing can be, should be, kept personal, private.

Success Criteria Matter

Each piece of student writing provides data for the student's skills and knowledge of the writing process. A piece of writing can be assessed individually or comparatively (i.e., a revised version of the original). Another model is to choose writing samples from early in a semester and compare it to student's writing at a later stage.

For each of the writing formats in this book, provide students with three success criteria to consider. Different formats address different expectations; by displaying and explaining criteria, students can determine how well they have done for a particular genre. Clear instructions and a consistent routine with self-assessment checklists can help to support and enrich young writers.

Process Matters

Writing is a process. Teachers may understand and implement the stages of writing—drafting, composing, revising, rethinking, redrafting, editing, and publishing—but writing never occurs in such neat phases. Students need regular and frequent time to draft if they are to learn the art and craft of writing. Often a piece that will eventually be published has to be set aside and developed at a future date. I'm reminded of my dear colleague Brian Crawford, who was concerned when teachers said, "Hand in your good copy." All copies, Brian claimed, were "good."

Across-the-Curriculum Matters

Although there is a need for a consistent, designated time within the literacy program for independent writing and writing workshop, students write throughout the day in school. It is recommended that we take note of the strategies they use as writers. Students can connect their writing projects in a variety of curriculum areas: recording observations in science and mathematics, using notebooks to record information in social studies and health, developing projects for individuals and groups in a variety of subject areas, writing in role in drama lessons. To value writing and consider authentic purposes for writing, students need to see themselves as writers outside of the language program and outside the classroom walls.

Consider Your Writing Program

Here are some questions to ask yourself about your current practices. Are you satisfied with your answers? How might these questions help you rethink, rework, and improve your practices?

- ☐ Do you have a writing period scheduled each day?
- ☐ How often do you present reading workshops with explicit instructions for demonstrations of genre-writing, craft lessons, revising and editing skills?
- ☐ Is there a balance between student choice and teacher assignment for writing projects?
- ☐ Is there a balance between writing fiction and writing information?
- ☐ Do students have opportunities to write independently, in pairs, and in small groups?
- ☐ Do you organize writing conferences to allow you to connect with each student weekly?
- ☐ Do you monitor each writer in order to give feedback and support when needed?
- ☐ Do you provide oral feedback to student writing?
- ☐ Do you provide written feedback to student writing?
- ☐ Do you use mentor texts to demonstrate the craft of writing?
- ☐ Do you provide students with opportunities to write in different subjects?
- ☐ How often do you provide opportunities for students to write in order to express and reflect upon their reading experiences?
- ☐ Do you encourage students to write outside of the classroom experience?
- ☐ Do you show students your own writing?
- ☐ Do your students have writing buddies?
- ☐ Do your students have different audiences, besides you, for their writing (e.g., peers, school community, families)?
- ☐ Do students have opportunities to publish their writing? How often?
- ☐ Do you provide prompts to motivate students?
- ☐ How important is talk in your writing program (before, during, and after writing)?
- ☐ What part does technology and/or the internet play in planning and developing student writing?
- ☐ How often is poetry writing introduced into the program?
- ☐ Do you have a successful program for using journals/notebooks?
- ☐ What opportunities do you have for writing in role or perspective writing?
- ☐ How comfortable are you with assessing student writing?

See Assessment Checklist on page 119.

The ABCs of Writing Lessons

Advertisements • Alphabet Books • Announcements • Autobiographies • **B**iographies • Blackout Poems • Book Blurbs • Brochures • **C**haracterizations • Character Journals • Cinquain Poems • Commercials • **D**efinitions • Dialogue • Diaries • **E**pilogues • Essays • Essays to Persuade • Excuses • **F**ables • Formula Poems • Four-Rectangle Response • Free Verse Poems • **G**lossaries • Graphic Texts • **H**aiku • How-To • **I**nterviews • **J**okes • Journals • **K**WL • **L**etters • Letters in Role • Letters to Persuade • Lists • List Poems • **M**emoirs • Mysteries • Myths • **N**ame Stories • Newsletters • News Reports • **O**bservations • **P**atterns • **Q**uestions • Quickwrites • Quizzes • Quotations • **R**eading Response Journals • Recipes • Recounts • Reviews • Rules • **S**cripts for Readers Theatre • Social Media • Surveys • **T**hank-You Messages • Thinking Stems • Titles • Transcriptions • **U**rban Tales • **V**oice • **W**ord Games • Word Power • Writing in Role • **X**pert Writing • **Y**arns • **Z**odiac

Advertisements

The goal of advertising is to persuade people to buy a certain product or to sell an idea. A successful ad—in a newspaper, magazine, billboard, or website—attracts attention with clever design or presentation, often using effective words or slogans to get across the message.

Read to Write: Investigating Ads

1. Find an ad in a newspaper, in a magazine, or online that you think is appealing. Consider:

   - What is it selling?
   - Who is the audience?
   - What words or phrases are used to get your attention?
   - How do font size, color choice, and arrangement of the words make this a successful ad?
   - Do visual images capture your attention?
   - Is the message clear? What questions do you have about this ad?

2. Meet in small groups to explain your choice and compare ads.
3. As a class, create and display a list of criteria that could be used to make a successful ad.

Write to Read: Creating Ads

1. Review the criteria for ads.
2. Complete a one-page ad for a product of your choice; for example, a toy, a game, food, an instrument, a clothing item, a backpack, a computer, a cell phone, a bicycle, etc.
3. Meet in groups to share ads. Discuss with your group what makes the ad successful, perhaps offer suggestions to be considered for revising the ad.

Writing Tip
A successful advertisement will draw attention through both words and pictures. How do font size, color choice, and arrangement of the words make your ad successful?

Let's Go Further: Classified Ads

Classified ads or *want ads* provide information about goods or services people wish to acquire. Traditionally they appeared in newspapers and were priced by the word, so they needed to include as many facts as possible in a few lines. Choose a topic from the list and prepare a classified ad that could appear in a newspaper or on the Internet:

- Wanted: Teacher
- Wanted: Babysitter
- Wanted: Dog walker
- Wanted: Veterinarian
- Wanted: Gardener

Alphabet Books

Alphabet Books, or ABCs, are usually based on theme or topic to give information with words and pictures, and to engage readers of all ages.

Read to Write: Investigating Alphabet Books

Share an alphabet book with your classmates. Some recommendations:

> *ABC x 3: English, Español, Français* by Marthe Jocelyn
> *A is for Activist* by Innosanto Nagara
> Bad Kitty series by Nick Bruel
> *Eating the Alphabet: Fruits and Vegetables from A to Z* by Lois Ehlert
> *Inclusion Alphabet: ABC's for Everyone* by Kathryn Jenkins

In groups of five or six, compare your books, focusing on the language pattern and how the author and illustrator have presented information alphabetically. Some patterns you might notice:

- One word per page: e.g., *Apples, Bananas, Cucumbers, Dates,* etc.
- Simple sentence: e.g., *A is for Aardvark.*
- Alliteration: e.g., *The lion lounges lazily near the little lake.*
- Names of people and/or places: e.g., *Alex lives in Alberta.*
- Feature word + information: e.g., *A is for Activist. An activist a person who campaigns to bring about social or political change.*

Write to Read: Creating an Alphabet Book

Writing Tip
In English, sometimes the letters *Q, X, Y,* and *Z* can be problematic. Try adding an adjective (e.g., a Yellow hat), or "bending the rules" of spelling (e.g., Xercise = Exercise)—or consider omitting these letters.

1. Working independently or with a partner, choose a topic of interest.
2. Brainstorm an alphabetical list of words about that topic.
3. Consider a repeated structure that will be followed for each page.
4. Prepare a draft copy of a 26-page alphabet book.
5. Ask for feedback from others to help clarify your ideas and edit for spelling and punctuation.
6. Prepare a final draft including illustrations.
7. Share the book with others, perhaps with a group of younger students.

Let's Go Further: Collaborative Alphabet Book

Alphabet books are ideal as collaborative books. Once a pattern is established and demonstrated, each of member of your class can create a page of the book. The book can be assembled into a 26-page product in which each student has contributed.

Announcements

An announcement is a public declaration of an event that has happened or will be happening.

Read to Write: A Birth Announcement

In her poem, "Hey World, Here I Am!" author Jean Little announces her own birth. Consider an announcement your family would send to let the world know about your birth. What might you like to announce to the world to let them know what you look like, what you feel like, what you wonder about, and what you hope to accomplish?

Write to Read: Writing an Announcement

Writing Tip

Announcements can be put on display on a bulletin board or presented orally for others to listen to. To determine how successful you were at preparing an announcement, practice reading the announcement out loud.

1. Choose one of the following topics:

Birth of a pet	Upcoming sports event
Upcoming bake sale	Congratulations to a winning team
Extracurricular meeting of a club	Weather report
Raffle or contest	School election
Fun fair	

2. Working in pairs, write an announcement of five sentences. Announcements should answer these questions: *Who? What? Where? When? Why?* and *How?*
3. Each partner reads aloud the announcement. Is all the important information given? Should any information be added? Left out? Does announcement get your listener's attention?

Let's Go Further: Announcements Aloud

Write an announcement to be shared during school announcements:

- A brother or sister for sale
- Birth of a dragon/sale of a dragon
- Arrival of an alien creature to Earth
- Proposed trip to outer space
- Proposed trip in a time travel machine
- Visit of a superhero to the school

Rehearse reading the announcement out loud. Can you share enough information in exactly one minute?

Autobiographies

An autobiography is someone writing about their own life. *Autobiography* comes from the Greek words *autos* (meaning "self") and *bios* (meaning "life").

Read to Write: An Autobiography Recommendation

Fatty Legs by Margaret Olemaun Pokiak-Fenton and Christy Jordan-Fenton is a powerful true story of Margaret's time in a Residential School in the Far North. Christy Jordan-Fenton is Margaret's daughter-in-law, who co-wrote this book told in the first person as Margaret's autobiography.

Write to Read: All About Me

Writing Tip
You might choose one of these three strategies to prepare to write the stories of your life:
- A timeline: year-by-year highlight of events
- A visual map: a life in pictures on chart paper or large sheet of construction paper
- A mind map: family, friends, school, hobbies, favorites

Use this plan to write an autobiography that will let others know about your life.

1. A paragraph about your past:
   - When and where were you born
   - Interesting things from your past

2. A paragraph about your family:
   - How many are in your family? Names?
   - Stories or facts about family members

3. A paragraph about your school:
   - Schools and teachers you remember
   - Subject interests; accomplishments

4. A paragraph with more about you:
   - Friends
   - Hobbies and pastimes
   - Favorites: color, food, sport, game, book, TV show, etc.

5. Consider including one or more of the following:
   - photographs or drawings
   - lists
   - an *I Am...* poem
   - mementos; e.g., artwork, possessions, good luck charms

Let's Go Further: Presenting Autobiographies

- *My Life In Pictures*: A collection of photos, presented chronologically with captions
- *My Life: People, Places, Things*: An alternative way to organize paragraphs
- *A Timeline*: Significant events from year to year
- *All-About-Me Picture Book*: Titles and subtitles can help organize
- Digital Story or Slide Show: Pictures with voice-over narration
- Alphabet Autobiography: Each page dedicated to a letter of the alphabet

Biographies

A biography is the life story of someone written by another person.

Read to Write: Picture Book Biographies

Picture books biographies present stories of a life through words and pictures:

- *Nelson Mandela* by award-winning author/illustrator Kadir Nelson: biographical sketch of South African President Nelson Rolihlahla Mandela, told in free verse and powerful illustrations.
- *Viola Desmond Won't Be Budged!* by Jody Nyasha Warner, illustrated by Richard Rudniki: narrative biography of the civil-rights activist who, in 1946, challenged racial segregation at a movie theatre in Nova Scotia.

Also recommended:

> *I Am Not a Label: 34 Disabled artists, thinkers, athletes and activists from past and present* by Cerrie Burnell; illus. Lauren Baldo
> *Rosa* by Nikki Giovanni; illus. Bryan Collier
> *Six Dots: A story of young Louis Braille* by Jen Bryant; illus. Boris Kulikov
> *Some Writer! The story of E.B. White* by Melissa Sweet
> *Unstoppable: Women with Disabilities* by Helen Wolfe; illus. Karen Patkau

Write to Read: Writing a Biography

Writing Tip
There are several ways you can present biographical information. You could
- use different headings on separate pages
- include copies of photographs and/or create illustrations to accompany your text
- outline highlights of the person's life as a timeline
- create a digital story or slide show of the person's life

1. Choose a remarkable person or someone that interests you to write a biography.
2. Prepare and develop your writing using texts from the library or information on the internet.
3. You could use these headings to organize your biography:

Birth and early childhood	Work experience
Education	Struggles and Accomplishments
Relationships	(Death)

4. More options for inclusion: famous sayings; what others have said about this person; adventures/anecdotes; a timeline; photographs or illustrations.

Let's Go Further

- You might choose to write a biography about someone you know; e.g., a relative, classmate, etc. An interview can help you gather information to add to information you already have about this person.
- As an alternative book report, you can write a fictional biography of a character in the book.

Blackout Poems

Blackout poetry is when a page of text—a newspaper article, for example—is blacked out except for a select few words that form a free verse poem. Backout poetry is a type of *found poetry* and is also known as reductive poetry or erasure poetry.

Read to Write: An Example of Blackout Poetry

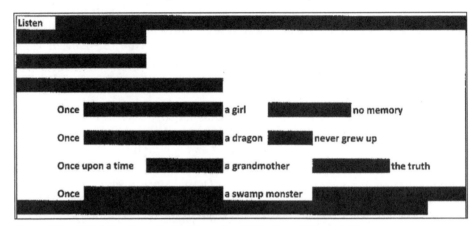

From *The Girl Who Drank the Moon* by Kelly Barnhill, p. 165

Write to Read: Creating a Blackout Poem

Writing Tip
You are encouraged to choose a number of words for your blackout poem; a maximum of 20 is a good place to start. Once you have gone through the blackout process, review the text at least one more time and continue to eliminate words.

1. Choose a piece of text: a newspaper article, a photocopied page from fiction or nonfiction, etc.
2. Skim the text.
3. Revisit the text and lightly circle words or phrases you want to use. It might be a good idea to set yourself a maximum so you don't "keep" too many words.
4. Go back through your poem and box the words you are keeping by blacking out everything else using a marker (a Sharpie is good), pen, or dark pencil. Review the text at least once to see if you can eliminate even more words.
5. Read through your final poem.
6. Meet with three or four classmates and share the process of creating your blackout poem. If you have used the same source text, compare your poems to see which words have been chosen by others.

Let's Go Further: Creating a Free-Verse poem

Create a free verse poem from words you think are essential to the meaning of your text by rewriting and formatting the words of your blackout poem.

Book Blurbs

A book blurb is a summary written to give readers just enough information to persuade them to read the book.

Read to Write: Investigating Book Blurbs

Find one or two paperback novels you haven't yet read. Examine the book blurbs on the back covers. Work in small groups to discuss the blurbs, considering what information has been provided about the plot, characters, and setting; what questions come to mind about the book; what predictions you have about the book; and what language was used to effectively lure readers to choose the book. Will you read the book based on the book blurb summary?

Write to Read: Writing a Book Blurb

Writing Tip

You and a classmate can write a blurb for the same book. Once completed, compare your work. The two of you might decide to collaborate to create a new piece by synthesizing ideas.

1. Use these criteria to create a book blurb for a novel you have enjoyed reading:

   - keep it short in length
   - describe central characters and their relationships to one another
   - highlight the major conflict
   - use attention-grabbing words and phrases
   - consider using questions and inviting readers to ask questions and make predictions
   - offer an opinion of why this book might appeal to readers

2. Work in pairs to share your book blurbs. How successful was your partner at meeting the success criteria for the book blurb?
3. You can post your blurbs on a class website to inform and invite others to read the recommended books.

Let's Go Further: The 200-Word Book Blurb

You are challenged to write a book blurb that is exactly 200 words in length. Continue to revise, edit, and choose only the best words to inform others about the book and motivate them to choose it to read.

A further challenge: The publisher is only allowing a book blurb that is 100 words in length. Revisit and revise your original summary to comply with this instruction.

Brochures

Brochures are a type of advertising that present essential information to customers or members of the public on the benefits that certain products or places can offer.

Read to Write: Brochure Hunt

Go on a hunt to find samples of brochures. Work in small groups to discuss them. Consider text features, such as titles, use of photographs or illustrations, maps, text boxes, use of color, use of different fonts and font size, etc. How successful is the brochure at presenting information?

Write to Read: Creating a Brochure

Writing Tip

There are a number of programs online that offer templates for making a brochure. Before using the computer, you can plan a draft of your brochure by considering not only the essential information that needs to be included, but also formatting (arrangement of words and visuals).

1. Gather and synthesize information and visual images to create a brochure to inform and persuade others about a service or place. You might choose to create a brochure to present information about a topic connected to a curriculum strand, for example:

   * city/country/landmark travel brochures (Social Studies, Geography)
   * the environment (Science)
   * the human body (Health)
   * health and safety: e.g., no smoking, eating well (Health)
   * a museum, gallery, theatre, or concert venue (the Arts)

2. Keep in mind these guidelines while planning and creating your brochure:

   * Write in short sentences.
   * Use bulleted lists.
   * Brochures are often presented as small tri-fold booklets. Make the first panel of your brochure the title page, the one that will be visible when the brochure is folded.
   * Include strong images—illustrations, photographs, maps, charts—to add visual appeal.
   * Consider how words and visuals will be arranged on a page.
   * Consider graphic design: the use of captions, titles, fonts, font sizes, colors.
   * Make your brochure as helpful as possible. What will readers learn? What action will be taken?

Let's Go Further: From Brochure to Presentation

You are invited to transform the information and images from your brochure into a PowerPoint or Prezi to share with the class. In this way, you can bring your brochure to life by outlining facts, offering opinions, and explaining essential information.

Characterizations

A writer makes characters come alive by telling what they look like, what they wear, how they speak, and what other characters say about them.

Read to Write: Collecting Characterizations

As you read novels, you will encounter vivid descriptions of characters. Collect these excerpts, using sticky notes to mark interesting descriptive passages.

Write to Read: Self-Portrait in Words

Writing Tip
Characterizations provide you a good opportunity to explore synonyms. Using a thesaurus can help you consider the best vocabulary to paint a picture of a character.

1. Write a paragraph about yourself that provides a detailed description of your physical self. This piece can be written in the first person (*My name is _____ and I would like to tell you about myself*) or third person (*Let me introduce you to…*).
2. Unlike autobiography, a self-portrait does not include past events or what you think or feel. Physical traits to include:

   Height
   Age
   Color of Hair
   Description of hair
   Description of nose, ears, mouth
   Voice
   Distinguishing features
   What you are wearing today

Let's Go Further: Inventing a Character

Find an illustration from a picture book or a photograph from a newspaper or magazine. Use the visual to invent details about this person. The goal of your writing is to make the characters come alive for your reader.

Character Journals

Character journals invite readers to imagine they are a character in a book they have read, and are written in the first person, using the pronoun "I."

Read to Write: How Journals Can Create Character

This student sample is from the point of view of Jonas in the novel *The Giver* by Lois Lowry.

> Dear Diary,
> Amazing day! In our black and white world I saw red. I am amazed by the colors that life offers. Then I started to think… Color? What does it mean… I asked my mom, "What does color mean?" She had a puzzled look on her face—as if she was waiting for this day to come. She stared back at me. She rubbed her head, pausing to think. Then she said "Sit down, Jonas…"

Write to Read: Journaling as a Character

Writing Tip
You can share your responses with others by working in role. Working in pairs, you can take turns interviewing a novel character.

1. Write a journal entry as a character in a novel. You can retell story events, discuss relationships with other characters, describe a problem and how/if it gets solved, and reveal the character's emotions.
2. The following list provides you with choices to consider for writing a character journal:

   - write a single entry or retell a series of events over time
   - write from the point of view of an animal or inanimate object
   - move forward in time to predict what might happen to a character after the novel ends
   - add illustrations or graphics

Let's Go Further: Perspective Writing in Different Media

Use your imagination and write one of the following:

- a letter, email, or text message from one character to another character in the same novel or to one from a different novel
- a social media post for a character in the story
- a newspaper, magazine, or media report about an incident or issue in the story

Cinquain Poems

A cinquain (SANG-kane) is an unrhymed shape poem composed of five lines, each with a special purpose.

Read to Write: Cinquain Poems

Examples of cinquain poems:

Pigeons	Goalies
Feathery, plump	Protecting, waiting
Flittering, fluttering, flying	Strong, cautious, attentive
Pecking all around	Always on the lookout
Pigeons	Goalies

Write to Read: Writing a Cinquain Poem About a Person

Writing Tip

Create two or three cinquain poems and then choose a favorite to publish in a class poetry book or to feature in a class blog. You may wish to illustrate your poem.

1. Use this pattern to create a cinquain poem:

   1st line: one word subject
   2nd line: two describing words about the subject (adjectives or –*ing* verbs)
   3rd line: three describing words about the subject (adjectives or –*ing* verbs)
   4th line: four-word phrase about the subject
   5th line: line one is repeated

2. Choose a person or character to write a cinquain poem about.
3. Once you have drafted your poem, share your poem with one or two classmates and discuss:
   - Has the writer followed the rules of writing a cinquain poem?
   - Have the best words been used to describe the topic?
   - What words or phrases might be changed?
4. Revise your poem, considering the feedback you have received.
5. Create two or three cinquain poems and then choose a favorite to publish in a class poetry book or to feature in a class blog.

Let's Go Further: Using a Syllable Pattern

You can use this formula to revise one of your poems or create a new poem on a topic of choice.

Line #1: Two syllables
Line #2: Four syllables
Line #3: Six syllables
Line #4: Eight syllables
Line #5: Repeats first line

Commercials

A commercial is a video advertisement aired on TV, on the radio, at a movie, or online to sell a product or inform an audience about a business or a service.

Read to Write: Viewing a Commercial

Work with a partner to find commercials on the internet about a product you find appealing. Share your choices and discuss the features that made each one a successful advertisement to motivate others to buy the product. Consider some of your favorite ads from TV, online, or from before a movie. What makes these commercials appealing? Motivating?

Write to Read: Creating a Commercial

1. Choose a product of interest to promote (e.g., sneakers, cereal, cookies, a video game, a restaurant, a website, etc.)
2. Write a paragraph to be the script for your commercial, using this outline:
   - What is the main idea you are presenting?
   - What information about the product can you provide?
   - How will the product be featured? Who will be in the commercial?
   - How will you begin your commercial to grab a viewer's attention?
   - How will you conclude your commercial to motivate viewers to buy the product?
3. You can share your commercial outline with a partner, in a small group, or with the whole class.

Let's Go Further: Creating a Commercial

Working alone or with one or two classmates, prepare a one-minute commercial and present it to others in the class. The outline that you have prepared can help you to create a commercial as dramatization or as a digital presentation. It is important to rehearse your presentation so you are comfortable sharing your work with an audience.

Definitions

A definition is a statement of the meaning of a word.

Read to Write: Investigating Definitions

The Merriam Webster dictionary defines the verb *to bully* this way:

> To treat someone in a cruel, insulting, threatening or aggressive manner.

Author Barbara Coloroso defines *bullying* in her book *The Bully, The Bullied, and The Bystander*:

> Bullying is a conscious, willful and deliberate hostile activity intended to harm, induce fear through the threat of further aggression and create terror.

> What are the differences between these two definitions? Do you feel one is more relevant to you?

Write to Read: Be a Dictionary Editor

Writing Tip

Dictionary definitions denote the part of speech of the word they are defining (i.e., noun, verb, adjective). When writing definitions, be clear whether the word is a noun, verb, or adjective You can add detail to a definition for a noun by providing an explanation of the verb or adjective form.

A new dictionary is about to be published, but some words have yet to be defined. As a dictionary editor you have been called upon for input.

1. Choose one of the following words: *bully, peace, friendship, racism, dreams, family, refugee.*
2. To begin, work independently. Use a file card or sheet of paper on which to write a personal definition of the word. There are no restrictions in length.
2. Meet with a partner to exchange definitions. Consider this question: What words or phrases from your partner's definition would you like to borrow to include in your definition?
3. Work together with your partner to synthesize definitions. You are encouraged to include words from each partner's definition and/or to add new words. Create a definition that is exactly 25 words in length.
4. Examine definitions from a dictionary or the internet to compare with your own.

Let's Go Further: Visual Definition

The new dictionary will be strictly visual, so all definitions must be represented without words. Work independently to create an image or design to represent what a bully is.

Dialogue

Dialogue is a conversation between two or more people as a feature of a book, play, or movie.

Read to Write: Picture Books Featuring Dialogue

Duck! Rabbit! by Amy Krouse Rosenthal; illus. Tom Lichtenheld
I Want My Hat Back by Jon Klassen
It's a Book! by Lane Smith
Yo! Yes? by Chris Raschka (also *Ring! Yo?*)

Write To Read: Telephone Dialogue

Writing Tip

Quotation marks let readers know something is being said by a character. Three essential rules for formatting dialogue:
1. Place all spoken words within quotation marks.
2. Punctuation that ends a sentence stays inside the quotation marks.
3. Use a new paragraph to indicate a new speaker.

1. In pairs, write a telephone conversation between two people. To prepare, have a short conversation using one of the following scenarios:

   - two friends arguing
   - a child requesting permission from a parent
   - seeking advice from a worker in a pet store
   - ordering food from a restaurant
   - a 911 distress call

2. Dialogues should be at least 15 lines in length. You do not have to include who is speaking. Readers will know from the information presented in the conversation.
3. Read your conversation out loud. Take turns reading each part to make sure ideas are clear.
4. Revise your conversation. What might be added to make the conversation more authentic?

Let's Go Further: Transforming Conversations

1. From Graphic Page to Dialogue: Choose a comic strip or graphic novel excerpt. Transform the speech balloons into dialogue. Use the exact words of the conversation.
2. From Dialogue to Graphic Page: Choose an excerpt from a novel that includes dialogue and transform it into a comic strip.
3. From Text Message to Dialogue: Transform a text conversation you have had with a friend into dialogue.

Diaries

Diary entries are personal, are often recounts of recent or past experiences, are presented chronologically, and should answer *who? what? where?* and *when?*

Read to Write: Diary Mentor Texts

- Author Doreen Cronin and illustrator Harry Bliss created a series of picture books that present diaries of the lives of various animals: *Diary of a Worm, Diary of a Spider, Diary of a Fly*.
- *The Diary of a Wimpy Kid* is a hugely popular fictional series by Jeff Kinney.

Write to Read: Keeping a Diary

Writing Tip

You may wish to own a diary and choose to write consistently, if not daily. In this way, writing becomes authentic, rather than an assigned task.

1. Consider these ideas for diary entries:

   - specific activities experienced through the day
   - something different or unusual that happened to you
   - interesting thoughts you had
   - important feelings
   - conversations
   - thoughts or predictions about tomorrow

2. Since diary writing is personal, you are invited to voluntarily share particular entries with your friends or teacher.

Let's Go Further: A Log

A log, like a diary, records events day-by-day, or over a certain period of time. In a log, dates or times can be featured to document observations. You might like to keep a log on one of the following items:

- the life of a puppy, kitten, or hamster
- the growth of a plant
- clothes worn each day
- the food and drinks consumed during a week
- the exercise you get
- a vacation
- the growth of a baby sister or brother

Epilogues

An epilogue appears at the end of a book. Usually a few pages in length, an epilogue often reveals the fates of the characters and wraps up any loose ends.

Read to Write: Some Novels that Have Epilogues

Finding Junie Kim by Ellen Oh
Goodbye, Mr. Terupt by Rob Buyea

Write to Read: Writing an Epilogue

Sometimes when we read a novel, we may not be satisfied with the way the author has concluded the story. Some questions remain in our heads.

1. Write an epilogue for a novel that you have read. You can

   - tell readers what happened to the character(s) after the story ended
   - push the narrative into the future (perhaps a day, or a year or years), perhaps confirming predictions that a reader might have in their head
   - hint at the possibility of a sequel where we might meet the characters again
   - emphasize an essential theme of the book and importance of what the story is about

2. Meet in groups to share your written work.

Let's Go Further: Writing a Prologue

A prologue is a separate introductory section that describes an event or action that has taken place in the past and leads to the events of the story. Usually short, a prologue can introduce characters and setting, and can hint at relationships and problems that will evolve in the novel.

Prepare a prologue that could introduce a novel you have enjoyed. A prologue should

- immediately hook the reader
- describe an experience by introducing characters and setting
- be short, and avoid providing a resolution
- invite the reader to ask questions and make predictions
- motivate the reader to continue reading the book

Essays

Essays provide you with an opportunity to express your thoughts and feelings about a topic that interests you. Essays can also include research information to support an idea or ideas.

Read to Write: Investigating Essays

To prepare to write an essay, you are invited to use the internet to find and read a short essay on a topic of your choice. You might also find an interesting essay in a magazine or as an appendix in a nonfiction picture book.

Write to Read: Writing an Essay

Writing Tip

Writing an essay helps to organize your thinking on a topic, usually by presenting the information in a number of paragraphs. This process helps you to understand the topic better and sort out any feelings you might have about it. When others read your essay, they come to know the topic better too.

1. Plan your essay by creating a point-form outline. You might use a five-paragraph format to help organize the information for the reader:

   1. Introductory Paragraph: The topic sentence states the main idea of the essay. In this paragraph, write two or three sentences to outline the process or what you have learned about the subject.
   2. Supporting Paragraph: Elaborates on the first step in the explanation or inquiry.
   3. Supporting Paragraph: Elaborates the next step in the explanation or inquiry.
   4. Supporting Paragraph: Finalizes the explanation or inquiry.
   5. Closing Paragraph: Summarizes the explanation or learning.

2. Using the point-form outline, prepare a draft copy of your essay.

Let's Go Further: Editing Groups

Giving and receiving feedback is important to help you revise and edit your essay. Organize yourself into editing groups with one or two classmates. Once draft copies of essays have been completed, writers can read the essay aloud or have a partner read it silently. Some questions to consider when giving feedback:

- What information did you learn by reading this essay?
- How did the essay reveal the author's personal connections to the topic?
- What did you learn about, wonder about, while reading this essay?
- Have ideas been presented clearly?
- What information could be deleted?
- Does the writer seem to have an audience in mind?

Essays to Persuade

Some essays are written to inform readers about a problem or issue and persuade them to act. Both reading and writing an essay can help you to understand an issue and clarify how you feel about it.

Read to Write: Investigating Persuasive Essays

To prepare to write a persuasive essay, you are invited to use the internet to find and read a short essay the author has written to share their point of view and attempt to challenge or affirm your assumptions about an issue or topic. You might find persuasive essays on such topics as healthy eating, mindfulness, climate control, book banning, gun control, etc.

Write to Read: Writing a Persuasive Essay

1. Choose a topic you believe in strongly.
2. Using the five-paragraph format, prepare a point-form outline for your essay.

   1. Introductory paragraph: In this paragraph, write two or three sentences. You could introduce the problem; tell why it is important to do something about it; share a personal reason for considering this topic.
   2. Supporting paragraph: Define the problem by homing in on the issue and explaining why it is a problem or why it is an important issue to consider.
   3. Supporting paragraph: Give further reasons why you are concerned about the problem, perhaps exploring what will happen if nothing is done. Consider including a quotation or reference by an expert to support your views.
   4. Supporting paragraph: This paragraph provides the opportunity to tell what can be done to solve the problem. You can provide two or more specific actions that could be taken to address the issue. Or an argument might be included that could lead into a fifth paragraph about taking action.
   5. Closing paragraph: In this paragraph, suggest to readers ways they can help. A conclusion might tell how the world will be better if the issue is addressed.

3. Using your point-form outline, prepare a draft copy of your essay.
4. Organize yourself into an editing group with one or two classmates. You can read your essays aloud or silently.
5. Use suggestions from the feedback you receive to prepare a final draft.

Let's Go Further: From Essay to Speech

Prepare your essay to give as a speech. What changes would you make to present the information orally? How will rehearsal help you to know the speech well? Will some parts be memorized? How will voice and gesture engage the audience?

Writing Tip

Persuasive essays are related to expository essays, which are intended to explain something. The writer attempts to make clear their understanding of a subject. An expository essay may explain a process or a situation, or tell how to do something.

Excuses

Excuses are made-up reasons we use to get out of doing something, or to get off the hook for not having done something we were expected to do.

Read to Write: The Dog Ate My Homework…

In the picture book *I Didn't Do My Homework Because…*, Davide Cali presents a list of humorous and absurd excuses for not doing homework: e.g., giant lizards invaded the neighborhood, elves ate all the pencils. What are some excuses you might give a teacher for not having completed your homework?

Write to Read: Writing Excuses

Writing Tip

You can create humor by exaggerating your excuses. For example, for getting out of practicing an instrument, consider: *I need to rest my fingers so I can be ready to write the test tomorrow; I want to keep things quiet so I won't wake up Grandpa.*

1. Brainstorm a list of excuses for getting out of doing something around the house; e.g., doing dishes, cleaning your room, taking the dog for a walk, helping put the groceries away, babysitting a younger sibling, practicing piano (or any other lesson).
2. Work with a partner to compile a written list of excuses for one of the following:

   - not studying for a test
   - staying home from school
   - avoiding a visit to a relative
   - refusing to eat a meal you don't like
   - not taking a bath or shower
   - not joining a sports team

3. Using one of your excuse lists, write a letter or email to a parent, neighbor, friend, or teacher to convince them that you can't meet a responsibility. You might have fun with clever excuses or instead seek understanding or forgiveness.

Let's Go Further: Excuses List Poem

Your can use your excuses to create a list poem. Your poem should list five or more excuses that you have brainstormed, perhaps arranged from the most believable to the most ridiculous.

Fables

Fables are short folktales that often use animals to represent certain human types and end in a simple moral or lesson.

Read to Write: Reading Fables

Author/illustrator Jerry Pinkney has written beautiful wordless picture books of two familiar fables in pictures only: *The Lion and the Mouse* and *The Tortoise and the Hare*. You can use one of these titles to write the words you think might accompany the illustrations.

Write to Read: Writing a Fable with a Moral

1. Select one of these morals to inspire the fable you will write:

Good things come in small packages.	Necessity is the mother of invention.
Things are not always what they seem.	Be content with what you have.
If at first you don't succeed, try, try again.	A bird in the hand is worth two in the bush.
Actions speak louder than words.	Slow and steady wins the race.

2. Consider what lesson is inherent within the selected proverb. What story might help teach this lesson?
3. To prepare for writing a fable, you might work with one or two classmates to orally invent a plot, or series of main events, that could be written into a story alone or collaboratively.
4. Write a fable introducing animal characters of your choice, including plot and setting, exploring a problem, and explaining how the problem was solved to teach the characters/the readers a lesson.

Let's Go Further: Writing, Illustrating, Dramatizing Fables

To further explore fables you can

- work in groups to dramatize your fable through improvisation or Story Theatre
- present your fable as Readers Theatre
- rewrite your fable in the first person
- transform your fable into a graphic story
- illustrate your fable as a picture book to share with younger children

Writing Tip

Consider the voice that you are using to tell this story. Is it told in the first person, from the point of view of one of the characters, or the third person, using the pronouns *he*, *she*, or *they*? To experiment with which voice works best for you, you can transform your fable from first person to third person, or from third person to first person.

Formula Poems

Formula poems have patterns, syllable counts, or specific metre or rhythm.

Read to Write: Examples of Formula Poems

Acrostic

Perfect words
Organized with care
Enchant your ear
Transform your world
Refresh
Your heart
—Sheree Fitch

Limerick

There once was a dancer named
   Clive
Who danced a hot salsa and jive
Until one night he tripped
He slid and he slipped
Now Clive's twisted by staying alive.
—Sheree Fitch

Rhyming Couplet

If I were a bird and a bird was me
He'd be writing this poem and I'd be up a tree.
—Larry S.

Write to Read: Writing Formula Poems

Writing Tip
You have opportunities, over time, to create different formula poems. You can then choose a favorite poem you have written and present a final copy, perhaps illustrated. A class poetry anthology can be created with each student in the class contributing at least one poem to the collection.

Use these guidelines to write formula poems:

Acrostic
- first letter of each line spells subject of poem
- every line tells something about the subject.

Limerick
- five-line poem; lines 3 and 4 are shorter
- AABBA rhyme scheme
- bouncy rhythm; usually humorous

Rhyming Couplet
- two-line poem or stanza
- the two lines have an end rhyme

Let's Go Further: Syllable Poems

- Sijo: Korean three-line syllable poem; each line has 14–16 syllables, for a total of 44–46 syllables
- Haiku: three-line syllable poem; the lines have 5–7–5 syllables
- Tanka: five-line syllable poem; the lines have 5–7–5–7–7 syllables
- Quatrain: four-line poem or stanza; usually rhymed, with AABB, ABAB, and ABCB being popular rhyme schemes

Four-Rectangle Response

Four-Rectangles is a graphic organizer for your responses after reading or listening to a text.

Read to Write: Recommended Picture Books for Four-Rectangle Response

Fox by Margaret Wild; illus. Ron Brooks
Out by Angela May George; illus. Owen Swan
The Day War Came by Nicola Davies; illus. Rebecca Cobb
The Doll by Nhung N. Tran-Davies; illus. Ravy Puth
The Other Side by Jacqueline Woodson; illus. E.B. Lewis

Write to Read: Having a Four-Rectangle Conversation

The activity allows you to silently have a conversation on paper.

1. Work in groups of three. Each member of the group has a blank piece of standard paper folded twice to make four numbered rectangular spaces; see the example in the margin.
2. In space 1 of your sheet, write a short response to the text. Consider what it reminded you of; share your opinion; raise questions or puzzles.
3. Exchange your organizer with another person in the group. Read the response in space 1, then write a response to it in space 2. What did the response in space 1 encourage you to think about? You can agree or disagree with what was written.
4. Repeat the activity. Exchange papers so that you have a new Four-Rectangle sheet where you can write a response in space 3. Make sure to connect to what has been offered in each rectangle.
5. Sheets are returned to the person who wrote the first response. Read all three responses on your sheet and write a new response in space 4.
6. In your group, discuss the text, using the written responses to frame the discussion.

Let's Go Further: Conversation on Screen

An alternative way to have a conversation without speaking is to send text messages or emails to a partner, responding to each other's statements or questions. You can respond to a text you have read or choose a topic you feel strongly about: e.g., *Dogs make better pets than cats*; *Plastic bottles should be abolished*; *Why is so much money spent on space travel?*

Writing Tips
- Sentence stem prompts can be used: e.g., *I believe…, I agree…, I'm reminded of…, I wonder…*
- Having three to four minutes for each written response encourages you to fill in the space with more than one thought.

Free Verse Poems

Free verse poetry lets a poet express feelings and ideas without being restricted by traditional rules of metre and rhyme. The writer of free verse develops a form for each poem written.

Read to Write: From Prose to Poetry

One way to create a free verse poem is to transform a descriptive selection from a piece of prose into free verse. The poem in the margin was created from this passage from *Eggs* by Jerry Spinelli:

> He opened his eyes and followed the river to the crown of the rising sun. It was crisp and sharp and beautiful and smooth as a painted egg. And changing by the moment.

He opened his eyes
and followed the river
To the crown
Of the rising sun
It was crisp
And sharp
And beautiful
And smooth as a painted egg.
And changing
By
The
m o m e n t

Writing Tip

Prepare drafts of your free verse poem before using the computer for your final draft. Once you have the words and phrases you wish to use, the computer can help you create indentations and line breaks, and use different fonts and font sizes to add variety.

Write to Read: Writing a Free Verse Poem

1. Choose a subject for a free verse poem. Here are some suggestions for poem topics: *About me; My room; My friend; My favorite meal; The tree in my yard; The thrill of the sport; My bicycle; My favorite toy or game; A dream*
2. Write down words, phrases, or sentences that describe your subject. Consider the most effective word choices to describe your topic.
3. Rework your words and phrases by thinking of synonyms. Consider using similes, metaphors, personification, alliteration, etc.
4. Set up the poem so that the main ideas are arranged in an interesting way. Focus on what you want to say and leave out unnecessary words.
5. Consider line breaks and indentations as you write each line. Consider the number of lines in your poem and the use of white spaces and fonts.
6. Use the computer to prepare a final draft of free verse poem, playing with line breaks, white spaces, and fonts.

Let's Go Further: Class Free Verse Novel

A free verse novel is a series of free verse poems presented in a sequence that builds a narrative. With the rest of your class, you can create a free verse version of a novel you have all read. Each of you chooses one or two pages of the novel to transform the text into a free verse poem. Once completed, the work can be compiled into a free verse version of the novel.

Glossaries

A glossary is an alphabetical list of words with brief explanations or definitions, found in or relating to a specific subject or text.

Read to Write: Investigating Glossaries

Many works of fiction or nonfiction present vocabulary that might be unfamiliar to you. These books include a glossary at the end of the book to efficiently explain terms that have been presented in the text:

A Forest in the City by Andrea Curtis; illus. Pierre Pratt
I Am Not a Label: 34 Disabled artists, thinkers, athletes and activists from past and present by Cerrie Burnell; illus. Lauren Baldo
On the Trapline by David A. Robertson; illus. Julie Flett
This Book is Anti-Racist by Tiffany Jewell; illus. Aurelia Durand
The Triumphant Tale of the House Sparrow by Jan Thornhill

Write to Read: Creating a Glossary

1. Create a glossary for either a novel you have read (fiction) or a topic you are researching in Science, Social Studies, or Health (nonfiction).
2. Choose at least ten words that you don't know or that are unusual or difficult.
3. Use information in the text and a dictionary to find definitions of your glossary words.
4. When compiling your definitions into a glossary, consider these points:

   - The words in a glossary are presented in alphabetical order.
   - Definitions are usually short should clearly explain the meaning of the word.
   - A definition might include a simple illustration to help explain the word.

5. Once your glossary is completed, share it with others. What words in their glossaries are new to you? Did you learn more about words that are familiar to you?

Let's Go Further: My Personal Glossary

This activity provides you with an opportunity to prepare a glossary of at least ten words about a topic of personal interest (e.g., baking, bicycle parts, internal body parts, fishing, gaming, gymnastics, tools, sewing, a favorite sport). Working alone or with a partner, use the internet to investigate a list of at least ten terms and their definitions. Present your glossary as a chart by listing the vocabulary term in the left column and the definition in the right column of a two-column table.

Graphic Texts

In graphic texts, a story is told in panels through illustrations, dialogue balloons, thought bubbles, and narrative captions. Graphic text genres include adventure, fantasy, realistic fiction, science fiction, history, and autobiography.

Read to Write: Investigating Graphic Texts

Some popular graphic novel series:

> Babymouse by Jennifer Holm; illus. Matthew Holm
> Bone by Jeff Smith
> Dog Man by Dav Pilkey (also Captain Underpants series; Cat Kid Comic Club series)
> Real Friends trilogy by Shannon Hale; illus. LeUyen Pham

Work with a partner to discuss the use of graphic text features, including the following:

- panels, panel borders
- narrative captions
- speech balloons, thought bubbles
- font choices
- points of view: close-up, middle-distance, long-distance/landscape

Write to Read: Creating a Graphic Text

Writing Tip
Graphic templates can be found on the internet. You can choose one or more of these graphic organizers to plan and develop a graphic story.

You can create your own graphic text in one of these ways:

- Presenting a knock-knock joke as a comic-strip panel
- Inventing a new comic strip featuring character(s) from a favorite comic strip
- Transforming a script or conversation into comic format
- Creating a graphic page or two to present biographical or autobiographical information
- Inventing characters, setting, and plot events for adventure, mystery, fantasy, or realistic fiction to create an original graphic story
- Transforming one or two pages of text from a novel into a graphic novel page of four to six panels that retells the story in comic format

Let's Go Further: Class Graphic Novel

As a collaborative project, your class can create a graphic novel of a favorite book you have all read. Each classmate can contribute a page or spread.

Haiku

Haiku poems use three lines of carefully chosen words to present a picture full of mood and feeling.

Read to Write: Investigating Haiku Poetry

Haiku most often follow a pattern of 17 syllables, with the first line containing 5 syllables, the second line containing 7 syllables, and the third line containing 5 syllables. Find and read some haiku. Some recommended collections of haiku:

> *Earth Verse: Haiku from the Ground Up* by Sally M. Walker; illus. William Grill
> *Guyku: A Year of Haiku for Boys* by Bob Raczka; illus. Peter H. Reynolds
> *H is for Haiku: A Treasury of Haiku from A to Z* by Sydell Rosenberg; illus. Sawsan Chalabi
> *My First Book of Haiku Poems: A Picture, a Poem and a Dream* transl. Esperanza Ramirez-Christenson; illus. Tracy Gallup
> *Whoo-ku Haiku: A Great Horned Owl Story* by Maria Gianferrari; illus. Jonathan Voss

How do these poems express a feeling about the world? What images and feelings has the poet created?

Write to Read: Creating Haiku Nature Poems

Haiku describe the world around us, and often express how we feel about nature and the environment.

1. Choose a nature topic, such as a season, landscape scene, or weather condition: e.g., autumn, a rainstorm, snowflakes, waves on a seashore, a river, forest, clouds, etc. Or you can use the haiku model to write a poem about an animal that interests you.
2. Write down a few words or phrases that tell something about your topic.
3. Revisit the list. Add words that paint a clear picture or appeal to different senses. Consider synonyms for your initial word choices.
4. Organize words in three lines, using the 5–7–5 syllable pattern.
5. Meet with one or two classmates to share your poems and discuss:

   - Has the writer followed the rules of writing haiku?
   - Have the best words been used to describe the topic?
   - What words or phrases might be changed?

Let's Go Further: Illustrating Haiku

You can illustrate a haiku you have written using a variety of media; for example, watercolor illustration, construction paper art, or torn-paper collage.

Writing Tip

You might challenge yourself to write a few different poems and then determine which is the most appealing.

How-To

How-to writing involves giving directions or outlining procedures for readers to follow.

Read to Write: Investigating How-to Books

Be You! by Peter H. Reynolds
Everyone Can Learn to Ride a Bicycle by Chris Raschka
How to Make an Apple Pie and See the World by Marjorie Priceman
How to Read a Book by Kwame Alexander; illus. Melissa Sweet

Are these how-to instructions easy to follow? They should be clear, accurate, and complete, with each step given in order.

Write to Read: How to Do Something You Can Do

Writing Tip
How-to instructions are easy to follow when they are clear, accurate, complete, and exact, and when they list each step in order.

Write instructions for something you are very familiar with; for example,

- How to tie a shoelace
- How to play a game of checkers
- How to get ready to go to school
- How to make a fruit kabob
- How to clean a hamster cage (or goldfish bowl)

1. Working in pairs, take turns giving instructions on your topic of choice. This will give you both a chance to consider information and steps required.
2. On your own, write down all necessary information in point form.
3. Review the list to consider what has been omitted and what is unnecessary.
4. Write the instructions in order. Use time-order words—like *first*, *then*, *now*, and *finally*—to organize the steps in the proper order.
5. Meet in pairs again to share your how-to. If directions are clear, your partner will not have problems carrying out the activity. If there is some difficulty, rewrite or expand instructions.

Let's Go Further: How to Get to School

Prepare a list of instructions on how to get to school from your home (or how to get home from school). To give complete clear directions for someone walking or riding a bicycle, include

- names of streets
- what turns to make
- signposts along the way
- how much time is needed
- how to identify the destination

You have the option of including a map with your directions.

Interviews

Interviews are arranged meetings in which someone is questioned for opinions or information.

Read to Write: *Dear Mr. Henshaw* by Beverly Cleary

In this novel, a sixth-grade boy presents a list of questions to interview his favorite author: e.g., How many books have you written? Where do you get your ideas? Do you like to write books? What is your favorite animal?

Write to Read: Conducting an Interview

1. Who do you want to interview? Interviews can be conducted with classmates, students in other classes, family members, neighbors, people in the community.
2. Why is this person being interviewed?

   - to gather a story or stories about their past
   - to gather information about a topic you are researching
   - to ask for an opinion (survey or questionnaire)
   - to seek information about a job, talent, hobby, or expertise

3. When will your interview be conducted? Arrange a time that best suits the interviewee.
4. What do you want to ask? Prepare a list of questions that could guide the conversation.
5. Will your interview be one-on-one or conducted by more than one person? Will you record the interview (the interviewee will need to grant permission)?
6. Once you have completed the oral interview, present it in writing using the interview format:

   Question: How long have you been working as a veterinarian?
   Veterinarian: I've been working in this kennel for 8 years.
   Q: Where did you get your training?
   V: I received a degree in veterinary medicine from a university in Maryland.

Let's Go Further: Interviewing in Role

Imagine you are interviewing a famous person you admire. Pretending you are a talk show, radio show, or podcast host, work in pairs to brainstorm ten or more questions that you might ask this person. Improvise a talk-show conversation between a host and the celebrity. The host asks prepared questions, but should be ready to raise new questions as the conversation unfolds. The person role-playing the famous person invents answers they think this person might give.

Writing Tip
The role of media reporter is a good choice to conduct an interview in role. In some cases, you can interview several people in related roles: e.g., inventors; people with the same job but different experiences; etc.

Jokes

Jokes, oral and written, are anecdotes told to cause amusement or laughter, especially a story that ends with a funny punchline.

Read to Write: Joke Books

Find a joke book or two to investigate different ways that jokes and riddles can be written. Notice the punctuation required for questions and answers.

Write to Read: Transcribing and Assessing Jokes and Riddles

1. Meet with five or six classmates for a joke-telling session.
2. Choose one or more of the jokes or riddles you told or heard that you found funniest.
3. When you write, your choice of joke will determine the format you use:

- a question-and-answer riddle usually requires 2 sentences—a question and an answer—that can be presented as conversation or script:

Q: Which city has the most eggs in the world?
A: New Yolk City.

- a knock-knock joke requires 5 sentences written as a dialogue

Knock! Knock!
Who's there?
Anita.
Anita who?
Anita use the bathroom. Please let me in.

- a riddle is a type of joke presented as a question and answer

Q: What do you call a monkey when you take away his bananas?
A: Furious George.

- some jokes are written/told as one liners, in which the beginning of the sentence sets up the premise and is followed by a punchline.

I thought I'd tell you a clever time-travel joke but you didn't get it!

Let's Go Further: Comic Strip Jokes

Decide how to transform a favorite joke or riddle into a comic strip. What characters will you include? How will you write dialogue? How will the joke be divided into panels?

Writing Tip
You can collaborate with the rest of your class to create a joke and riddle anthology, with each of you transcribing and illustrating a joke or riddle.

Journals

Journals can come in all shapes and sizes.

Read to Write: Books Featuring Journal Writing

Amelia's Notebook (series) by Marissa Moss
Dear Mr. Henshaw by Beverly Cleary (Sequel: *Strider*)
Isaiah Dunn is My Hero by Kelly J. Baptist
The Length of a String by Elissa Brent Weissman

Write to Read: Journal Options

1. Choosing what to write in your journal is essential. Some journal topics:

   - book reviews
   - bucket-list goals
   - dreams
   - emotions
   - exercise journal
   - food journal
   - hobbies
   - I wonder…
   - movie reviews
   - nature observations
   - plans (e.g., for a party)
   - poems
   - resolutions
   - sports
   - stories
   - TV log
   - travel
   - unsent letters
   - word collecting

2. You can pass on your journal to others, designating which page(s) you would like them to read. It is important that those who read your journal entries offer oral or written feedback to your writing.

Let's Go Further: Guided Journals

You can purchase a commercial notebook with blank pages for you to fill in by responding to specific prompts. Such resources can motivate you to write entries in response to suggestions: e.g., *What is the best vacation you've had? What do you think life might be like for you in ten years? Tell about a time you had an argument with a friend.*

Writing Tips

- Diaries differ somewhat from journals: the main focus of a diary is to record events that have happened in the writer's life and to reflect on these events.
- *Writing Radar: Using Your Journal to Snoop Out and Craft Great Stories* by Jack Gantos encourages readers and writers to search the everyday world for inspiration for journal writing.

KWL

What I/ we **K**now	What I/we **W**onder about	What I/we **L**earned

KWL helps you to combine background knowledge with new information about a topic.

Read to Write: Know/Wonder/Learn

Though ideal for exploring nonfiction texts, KWL can also be used to uncover information inherent in narrative stories, especially tough topics that will be explored over time: e.g., the Residential School experience, the Holocaust, mental health, climate change, prejudice and discrimination. Some recommended picture books on complex issues:

> *The Day War Came* by Nicola Davies; illus. Rebecca Cobb (refugees)
> *The Other Side* by Jacqueline Woodson; illus. E.B. Lewis (segregation)
> *Stolen Words* by Melanie Florence; illus. Gabrielle Grimard (Residential School experience)
> *The Orange Shirt Story: The True Story of Orange Shirt Day* by Phyllis Webstad; illus. Brock Nicol (Residential School experience)
> *When We Were Alone* by David A. Robertson; illus. Julie Flett (Residential School experience)

Write to Read: Using KWL to Organize Information

1. You can work on the KWL strategy using three columns as a graphic organizer independently, with a partner, or in small groups.
2. The KWL strategy traditionally is presented as a three-column graphic organizer:

   What I/we **K**now (activating prior knowledge)
   What I/we **W**onder about (questions)
   What I/we **L**earned (research)

3. Use the chart before, during, and/or after reading. New questions and new information can be added to the chart through a variety of resources you experience as your inquiry unfolds.

Let's Go Further: Large Chart

Sticky notes can be used to facilitate KWL strategy. Using color-coded sticky notes, you can flag

1. facts that you knew before reading the selection
2. questions you have about a topic
3. facts you have learned from research

Writing Tip
KWL strategy is ideal for gathering research on the life of an animal (e.g., loons, bats, jellyfish, honeybees), inspiring you to find picture books, nonfiction resources, and information on the internet that will help you answer questions.

Letters

Writing a letter to someone is often like talking to them; no matter the occasion, your can tell things you've done, how you are feeling, plans you have, or opinions or issues of concern. *Epistolary* describes a literary work presented in the form of letters.

Read to Write: Picture Books Written as Letters

Click, Clack, Moo: Cows That Type by Doreen Cronin; illus. Betsy Lewin
The Day the Crayons Quit by Drew Daywalt; illus. Oliver Jeffers
Dear Mrs. LaRue: Letters from Obedience School (series) by Mark Teague
I Wanna Iguana by Karen Kafuman Orloff; illus. David Catrow (also *I Wanna New Room*)
Please Write Soon: An Unforgettable Story of Two Cousins in World War II by Michael Rosen; illus. Michael Foreman
The Jolly Postman by Janet and Allan Ahlberg

Write to Read: Writing and Sending Letters to Someone You Know

Writing Tip: Letter-Writing Checklist
☐ Did I include a date on the top right side?
☐ Did I use an appropriate salutation?
☐ Did I check for spelling and punctuation?
☐ Did I convey my message clearly by stating opinions, retelling events, asking questions?
☐ Did I include a suitable closing before my signature (e.g., *Yours truly, Love, Sincerely*, etc.)?

1. Who are you writing to? It could be a friend, a relative, a teacher, school support (secretary, custodian, administrator, classroom volunteer, cafeteria staff), a pen pal, an author.
2. Occasions for letter-writing include telling news, giving thanks, sending best wishes, hoping the recipient gets well soon, apologizing, sympathy, etc.
3. Text features to include when writing personal letters.

   - Date
   - Salutation
   - Variety in sentences: statements, questions, exclamations
   - Paragraph indents
   - Closing
   - Signature

4. Personal letters might need to look personal. Your letters can use special stationery, be presented in handwriting, include illustrations.
5. If your letter is to go by snail mail, you need put it in an envelope with the name of person receiving the letter and their address, including the number and street name, the city, the province or state, and the postal code. Your return address can go in the top left-hand corner of the envelope. A stamp might be needed.

Let's Go Further: I Wish My Teacher Knew

Third-grade teacher Kyle Schwartz gave this statement to her students to finish:

I Wish My Teacher Knew…

In a safe environment, students opened up about their anxieties, fears, grief, challenges, hopes, and dreams. You can participate by writing letters to your teacher. that will be will be kept confidential, or can be presented online anonymously.

Letters in Role

Writing letters in role invites writers to pretend to be someone else and send correspondence to another person. By stepping into the shoes of a fictional character, you can send a message from that person's point of view and recount events or present a problem.

Read to Write: A Sample Letter in Role

Dear Miss Muffet,
I am sorry to have frightened you today in the woods but I was rather hungry and the smell of your curds and whey appealed to me. Were you surprised to see me or are you frightened by spiders? I'm really not that bad, once you get to know me (and feed me).
Yours truly,
Spider

Write to Read: Fictional Letter Writing

Writing Tip
Letter writing is an authentic form of writing, as there is an audience (real or implied). Who will be reading this letter? Why?

Step into the shoes of a story character to write a letter.

1. First, choose the character you will be writing your letter in role as. It could be

    - nursery rhyme or fairy tale character
    - a picture-book character
    - a fictional or real animal
    - a novel character writing to another
    - a historical figure
    - an alien creature

2. To prepare to write, consider

    - Who might this character be writing to? Why is the character writing?
    - What information from the story will you include in the letter?
    - What problem will be shared? What emotions will be conveyed?

3. When you write your letter, make sure the necessary features of a letter are in place: date, salutation, sentences and paragraphs, closing, and signature.
4. Once your letter is complete, exchange letters with a partner. After reading your partner's letter, you can reply to the letter in role.

Let's Go Further: Letter to an Alien

Using the picture book *If You Come to Earth* by Sophie Blackall as inspiration, quickwrite letters to an alien describing what life on Earth is like. You can use the author's beginning to inspire your writing:

Dear Visitor from Outer Space,
If you come to Earth, here's what you need to know about…

Letters to Persuade

Persuasive letter-writing encourages you to state a position and justify it.

Read to Write: Picture Books with Persuasive Letters

Click, Clack, Moo! Cows That Type by Doreen Cronin; illus. Betsy Lewin
The Day the Crayons Quit by Drew Daywalt; illus. Oliver Jeffers
Dear Mr. President by Sophie Siers; illus. Anne Villeneuve
I Wanna Iguana by Karen Kaufman Orloff; illus. David Catrow (also *I Wanna New Room*)

Write to Read: Writing as an Object

Writing Tip
Writing a letter to an editor of a newspaper, magazine, or school newsletter provides you with an authentic audience for persuasive letter writing in which you can share your opinions about a topic or issue.

The Day the Crayons Quit by Drew Daywalt is the story of a box of crayons gone rogue. In a series of hilarious letters to Duncan, the owner of the box, each crayon explains their concerns, frustrations, and call to action in a persuasive manner. Use Daywalt's title as an inspiration to write a first-person persuasive letter:

- Choose to become any color in the crayon box and complain to Duncan
- Imagine that you are a classroom item (e.g., eraser, stapler, desk, computer) and convince a student you should be treated better
- Write as a piece of abused sports equipment, an unused musical instrument, or an item of clothing that is no longer worn.
- Think of a toy or possession you once loved but which you have mistreated or abandoned. Write as the toy to say you are not happy and persuade your owner that you deserve more respect and attention.

Let's Go Further: Authentic Persuasive Letter Writing

You can develop persuasive writing skills by writing—and sending—letters about a real-life situation you care about to a school administrator, a politician, or someone in the community. Share your concerns and present arguments about issues that need to be addressed or things that need to be changed (e.g., bullying policies, vandalism, litter, environmental issues, etc.). Letters can be written as a call to action in response to newspaper or media reports: e.g., people having different views about wearing masks during the COVID-19 pandemic; an environmental issue of concern; a problem in the community (housing, transportation, pollution, etc.).

Lists

A list is a series of words selected by a writer for a particular purpose. A list can be arranged consecutively, chronologically, or randomly.

Read to Write: Listing What You Read

Create a list of ten books you have enjoyed reading. Identify three favorite titles and put an asterisk beside the one title that can be considered our all-time favorite.

Some books that feature list-writing:

The Curious Book of Lists by Tracey Turner and Caroline Selmes
Finding Kindness by Deborah Underwood; illus. Irene Chan
My Listography: My Amazing Life in Lists (fill-in-journal) by Lisa Nola;
   illus. Nathaniel Russell

Write to Read: A List Race

Writing Tip

Once your list is completed, review list words and use a dictionary to correct the spelling of some words. Are all items with titles capitalized? Are plurals used correctly?

1. Work in small groups of three or four. As a group, choose a topic from this list:

All the people in my life   Names of birds (or mammals)
Things we can read   Two-syllable color words (or food
Things that have numbers   words)
My ideal shopping list

2. List as many items as you can in 2 minutes.
3. Compare lists with group members: Who has the longest list? Which items were unique to your list? Which items were included by all members?

Let's Go Further: ABC Collaborative Lists

Work in pairs to prepare an alphabetical list on one of these topics:

- Things we write
- Names for a dog (or cat)
- Cities of the world
- Words to describe a friend
- Mammals
- Colors
- Things you'd find at a school

You can list more than one item for each letter of the alphabet. Challenge yourself to find words for the letters Q, X, Y, and Z, perhaps with the help of a dictionary. Meet up with another pair who has prepared a list on the same topic. What words on the list are similar or different?

List Poems

Following a syntactic pattern can turn an ordinary list into poetry.

Read to Write: *The Important Book*

Read *The Important Book* by Margaret Wise Brown and write your own The Most Important list poem. Choose a topic of interest and list five facts about it using this model:

The important thing about _____ is_____.

The last line repeats the statement made in the first line:

But the most important thing about _____ is _____.

Write to Read: I Am… List Poem

Writing Tip

Once your draft of a list poem has been prepared, experiment with the order of items and determine which items should begin or end the poem.

1. Choose from the list of sentence stems. It is suggested you prepare a list of ten items, but you can decide the length of your poem.

I am…	I like…	I respect…
I dream…	I try…	I hear…
I read…	I enjoy…	I can…
I have…	I believe…	I hope…
I wonder…	I wish…	I feel…
I remember…	I want…	

2. To create the poem, you can repeat stems; arrange statements in any order you think works best; repeat the first line of the poem at the end of your poem for effect.
3. Once the first draft is completed, revise your writing by including vivid adverbs, adjectives, and synonyms.

Let's Go Further: What Is It? List Poem

List 5 to 8 describing words that tell about your subject, which is not revealed until the last line of the poem. Consider appealing to the five senses (sight, sound, smell, touch, taste).

orange	
crackling	croaking
smoky	sleepy
mysterious	slimy
fire	frog
green	

Memoirs

A memoir is a written memory of an incident in our lives.

Read to Write: Memories of Kindness

When we read we often make text-to-life and text-to-self life connections. Pay attention when something you are reading triggers a memory that can be written as memoir. The picture books listed here tell stories about being kind. Might you have a personal memory about a time someone was kind to you? Or you were kind to someone?

> *The Day You Begin* by Jacqueline Woodson; illus. Rafael López
> *Each Kindness* by Jacqueline Woodson; illus. E.B. Lewis
> *Frog and Toad Are Friends* by Arnold Lobel
> *Sidewalk Flowers* by JonArno Lawson; illus. Sydney Smith
> *A World of Kindness* by editors and illustrators of Pajama Press

Write to Read: Writing a Memoir

Writing Tip
Sharing stories orally with others can be a meaningful preparation for writing since it helps you think about the events, the setting, the order of events, vivid details and emotions associated with the story. Following the conversation, you can write a memoir inspired by the story you shared out loud.

1. Think of a story from your own past. What is the first thing that you remember? Have you heard favorite stories from your families about when you were younger? Did anything happen to you in the past month or year that hold a special place in your life?
2. Turn and talk to one or two classmates to exchange personal stories that come to mind. As you listen to others tell their stories, are you reminded of stories from you own life?
3. Write a memoir inspired by the story you shared.

Let's Go Further: From Word to Story

Every word is a story. For this activity, let one or more single words inspire a memoir. Use the From Word to Story: An ABC list to find a single word that inspires a personal connection and can lead to ideas for action or emotions to write a memoir story. Alternatively, you may choose to combine any two or three words from different columns.

Mysteries

There are many types of mystery stories: stories about crimes, missing characters, the sudden appearance of strange objects or characters, or people being pursued.

Read to Write: *The Mysteries of Harris Burdick* by Chris Van Allsburg

This picture book consists of a series of images, ostensibly created by Harris Burdick, a man who has mysteriously disappeared. Each image is accompanied by a title and a single line of text that encourage readers to create their own stories. What story ideas do these titles inspire?

Another Place, Another Time   A Strange Day in July
Uninvited Guests   The Third Floor Bedroom
Missing in Venice

Write to Read: Whodunit?

Writing Tip

While writing, try to create suspense by providing the reader with clues about what will happen without giving everything away. Consider using foreshadowing, a literary device in which a writer gives a hint of what is to come later in the story. This makes the reader interested in, even guessing about, what will happen next.

1. Choose one item from each column.

Suspect	Setting	Object	Problem
a millionaire	crowded attic	empty chest	theft
a stranger	empty cellar	expensive jewelry	missing person
a recluse	haunted mansion	old map	sudden death

2. Use the elements to create a story that keeps readers guessing who did what and trying to solve the mystery.

Let's Go Further: Give Me a Clue

Work in groups of four or five, with each member finding one or two photographs from newspapers or the internet. Alternatively, each group member can bring in an object. Imagine that you are detectives who have been hired to solve the disappearance of a missing person. The photographs or objects are clues to the life of this person. Discuss how the clues can be interpreted and write a detective report or an article for the newspaper with your conclusions.

Myths

Myths are stories about gods and supernatural beings, told in the distant past to explain natural phenomena, forces that affect people, and problems involved in relationships.

Read to Write: Reading Myths

Some collections of myths from different cultures:

> *D'Aulaires' Book of Greek Myths* by Ingri d'Aulaire and Edgar Parin d'Aulaire
>
> *Gods and Goddesses of Ancient Egypt: Egyptian Mythology for Kids* by Morgan E. Moroney
>
> *Greek Myths* by Marcia Williams (graphic text)
>
> The Heroes of Olympus (series) by Rick Riordan

Write to Read: Writing a Myth

Writing Tip

If you are struggling to create an original myth, you can use a familiar myth as a source for writing.

1. Imagine you live in an ancient society concerned with something happening in the environment; e.g., rivers drying up; earthquakes (or thunderstorms); the bees have stopped making honey; the gradual disappearance of tigers (eagles, whales); etc.
2. Use these questions to write a myth to explain what is happening:

   - Where does your story take place?
   - What is the problem?
   - How is a supernatural/god involved?
   - What is your warning for future generations?

Let's Go Further: Legends

A legend is less concerned with the supernatural than myth, and often concerns a real person, event, or place. Legends can explain a belief or something in nature; describe an adventure; and/or include magic. Choose one of the following topics to invent a legend:

How snowflakes came to be

How stars were born

How birds learned to sing

How mountains were made

How islands were formed

How flowers got their smell

How clouds learned to make rain

How the giraffe got its long neck (or the elephant its trunk)

Name Stories

Everyone has a name. Behind every name is a story.

Read to Write: Reading Name Narratives

Alma and How She Got Her Name by Juana Martinez-Neal
My Name is Yoon by Helen Recorvits, illus. Gabi Swiatkowska
The Name Jar by Yangsook Choi
Thao by Thao Lam
Your Name is a Song by Jamilah Thompkins-Bigelow; illus. Luisa Uribe

What information did you learn from the story? What questions might you still
have about the name?

Write to Read: Writing Your Own Name Narrative

Writing Tip
When meeting in groups to share
name stories, discuss:
• What are some commonalities in
the stories we heard?
• What are some surprises we
encountered in our shared stories?
• What do name stories tell us about
equity and diversity?

1. Answer completely as many questions as you can from the What's Your
   Name handout. This can help you reflect on different aspects of your first,
   middle, and/or last name.
2. Meet in groups of five or six. Each of you should have a chance to tell a story
   about your name. Use your answers to guide your storytelling.
3. Discuss:

   • What are some commonalities in the stories we heard?
   • What are some surprises we encountered in our shared stories?
   • What do name stories tell us about equity and diversity?

4. Gather as a class, perhaps sitting in a circle. Taking up to one minute, tell the
   whole class group a story about your name.
5. Write a name story using information you shared with others.
6. Record a short story (two or three essential statements) about your name to
   contribute to a class digital presentation.

Let's Go Further: Investigating Name Stories

Interview family members, neighbors, or members of the school community to
investigate the stories behind their names. You can use interview techniques to
help with this inquiry project. Stories can be written as a narrative or presented
in the interview format.

Newsletters

A newsletter is a tool used to share relevant and interesting information with an audience. A classroom newsletter can be sent to your families to summarize curriculum events, share student work, make announcements, and give shout-outs to classroom events and accomplishments of students in your class.

Read to Write: Investigating Newsletters

Collect samples of class newsletters from other classrooms. Perhaps a younger or older brother or sister can share a newsletter from their class. What elements do all or most of the newsletters have in common? What parts are specific to just one newsletter?

Write to Read: Creating a Class Newsletter

Writing Tip
A number of free templates are available on the Internet for you to use to plan and create a weekly/monthly newsletter.

1. Work together as a class to decide on content for your newsletter. Content for class newsletters, usually made available digitally on a class website or blog, can vary from month to month. Consider:

   - an overview of curriculum strands (e.g., *In Math we are learning…*; *In Social Studies, we are exploring…*)
   - activities and projects the class is working on
   - literature that has been shared (e.g., read-alouds, literature circle novels)
   - congratulations on accomplishments (e.g., winning teams, awards)
   - future plans (e.g., trips, projects, assemblies)
   - fundraising initiatives (classroom or school-wide)
   - samples of student work
   - an interview with a student or school staff member
   - important dates to remember (e.g., class excursion, PD days)
   - jokes or riddles
   - comic strips
   - word puzzles

2. Consider organizing yourselves into teams of newsletter editors to complete tasks (illustrators, copy editors, formatting the newsletter, etc.). Each month, different students can be responsible for different tasks.

3. Make sure that everyone in the class appears at least once in every newsletter. A special feature can list names alphabetically and demonstrate how each one of you has participated: For example,

   - We collected these interesting words this month…
   - Our favorite books this month are…
   - Some things we learned this month…

Let's Go Further: Beyond the Classroom

To extend the classroom newsletter experience, investigate and report on events taking place in your grade division or within the school community.

News Reports

News reports, or current events, are about people, places, and things, and outline events and issues that are tragic or entertaining.

Read to Write: News Reports in Picture Books

The Breaking News by Sarah Lynne Reul
I Can Write the World by Joshunda Sanders; illus. Charly Palmer
The Nantucket Sea Monster: A Fake News Story by Darcy Pattison; illus. Peter Willis
On the News: Our First Talk about Tragedy by Dr. Jillian Roberts; illus. Jane Heinrichs (nonfiction)

Write to Read: Extra! Extra! Read All About It!

Writing Tip

As you prepare a news report, keep in mind that a successful news report should be brief, factual, and accurate.

1. Write a news report about a classroom, school, or community event. It could be World News, National News, Local News, Entertainment, or Sports.
2. Consider the components of a successful news report. Answer the six questions of good reporting as you collect and organize your information:

   1. Who is involved?
   2. What happened?
   3. Where did it happen?
   4. When did it happen?
   5. Why did it happen?
   6. How did it happen?

3. Make your report stronger by including

   - a headline that contains strong adjectives, action words, alliteration, and names of people and places.
   - an illustration or a photograph

Let's Go Further: Fictional News

- Write a news report about event within a novel you are reading.
- Write a fictional news report on a strange or preposterous event from your imagination. Some possible headlines:

Aliens Arrive

The Siting of the Sasquatch

The Day the Animals Escaped from the Zoo

The Return of the Dinosaurs

Yes, There's a Pot of Gold at the End of the Rainbow

Observations

Observations are a record of things we encounter in our everyday lives.

Read to Write: Outdoor Observations

Several picture books were written during the COVID-19 pandemic lockdown, when we were required to stay indoors. These titles tell stories about the need to pay attention and observe and respect the world outside our windows.

Outside In by Deborah Underwood; illus. Cindy Derby
Outside, Inside by LeUyen Pham
Outside, You Notice by Erin Alladin; illus. Andrea Blinick

Write to Read: Making and Writing Observations

1. Pay attention to everyday events in the classroom, in the school yard, in the community, and at home.
1. Make jot notes of descriptive details of what you see and hear. Notes can be a bulleted list.
2. Meet in groups of four or five to report your observations. Group members can ask questions to make you think about further details.
3. Use one of these topics as a source for observation writing:

Our Garden	Our Neighborhood Store
The Cafeteria	Outside My Window
The Gym Equipment Cupboard	Welcome to Our Refrigerator
The Closet in my Bedroom	Up in the Attic/Down in the Cellar

You might recall information from memory, but first-hand research will allow more detail.

5. Add details to your writing through

- careful choice of adjectives and adverbs
- use of synonyms
- use of metaphors
- use of adverb phrases
- appeal to senses (sight, sound, touch, and sometimes taste)

Writing Tip

The following suggestions may help you add details to help readers appreciate what was being observed:
- careful choice of adjectives and adverbs
- use of synonyms
- use of metaphors
- use of adverb phrases
- appeal to senses (sight, sound, touch, and sometimes taste)

Let's Go Further: Observing Visual Images

Choose a photograph from a magazine, an illustration from a book, or an image of a work of art. List ten to twelve features to describe the image. Provide enough detail so that a reader gets a good sense of what you have observed. Work in pairs to exchange writing (without presenting the image). Can you guess what is happening in the picture? Which details are the most striking? Would you be able to create a drawing by reading your partner's written observations? As a follow-up, show the picture to your partner to see how complete your written observations were.

Patterns

Pattern stories follow a sequential pattern that is repeated throughout the book.

Read to Write: Investigating Pattern Books

Author/illustrator Todd Parr follows a distinct simple pattern based on a theme in each of his books: *It's Okay to Be Different*; *The Peace Book*; *The Kindness Book*; *The Thankful Book*; *Reading Makes You Feel Good*. Here is a suggestion: when reading a patterned story or poem, consider

- what words are repeated
- if the sentences are similar in length and form
- if the pattern remains the same throughout or if the author changes the way ideas are presented
- if there is a rhyming pattern

Write to Read: Patterns for Writing

Writing Tip
Picture books are often used as sources of patterns, and it is important to explore the repeated syntactic pattern that an author has used and you can imitate.

1. *Would You Rather…* by John Burningham:

   Would you rather your house was surrounded by water, snow, or jungle?

   Write and illustrate your own Would You Rather…: e.g., *Would You Rather buy…; read…; discover…; be chased by…; live with…; visit…; eat…*; etc.

2. *One Day, The End* by Rebecca Kai Dotlich; illus. Fred Koehler. For each story, the author provides a topic sentence, gives one narrative sentence, fills in details with illustrations, and concludes with the words "The End." For each story, write at least three sentences to explain what happens between the beginning and the end. Try writing and illustrating your own very short story.

3. *Read Anything Good Lately?* by Susan Allen and Jane Lindaman; illus. Vicky Enright. Working alone or with a partner, use this pattern to complete the alphabet:

   An atlas in the attic   A biography in bed

4. *Sometimes I Feel Like a Fox* by Danielle Daniel. Write your own animal descriptions using this pattern:

Sometimes I feel like a bear,	(animal)
Strong and confident,	(two adjectives)
I stand tall and growl	(fact written in the first person)
And protect those around me.	(fact written in the first person)

Let's Go Further: Collaborative Book

Write one page based on a pattern that the class decides on. Use the writing process to draft, revise, and edit your page; create an illustration to accompany your text. When the final version of all pages are ready for publication, the pages are collected and/or transformed into digital format or ebook.

Questions

Questions are the stuff of curiosity, imagination, and inquiry. Questions can spur us to seek out answers and to add information to our bank of knowledge.

Read to Write: Questioning as a Comprehension Strategy

When we read, we often become curious about what is happening, what might happen, and what will happen. Our questions can spur us on to continue reading. You can

- work with others to brainstorm questions you have before reading a text
- use sticky notes to record questions you have during the reading
- develop questions you might ask a character
- develop questions you might ask the author of a book

Write to Read: Brainstorming Questions

1. Imagine you and some classmates are media reporters who will interview a time traveller.
2. In groups of three, brainstorm questions you might use in an interview.
3. Use your questions to conduct a talk-show interview with one of these characters.

An award winning chef (or baker)	An undertaker
A wizard	A shark expert
A toy or game inventor	A ghostbuster
An astronaut	Harry Potter
An alien visitor	Little Red Riding Hood
A circus owner	

One person assumes the role of the character, and one or more people can ask questions.

Let's Go Further: Question Matrix

The Question Matrix lets you explore question stems and consider different types of questions, from simple, literal thinking to higher-level, inferential thought. Using the Question Matrix chart, form questions by using words from the left-hand side of the sheet and combining them with words at the top of the page. Choose one of the following sources to build questioning:

- picture book illustration (e.g., *The Arrival* by Shaun Tan; *The Mysteries of Harris Burdick* by Chris Van Allsburg)
- photograph
- character from a novel
- historical figure
- animal
- collection of objects that can lead to finding a missing person

Quickwrites

For quickwrites, you respond to a question or topic in a short period of time (five to ten minutes), letting your thoughts flow freely onto the page without addressing spelling or making revisions.

Read to Write: Books with Titles or Leads that Can Inspire Quickwrites

The Boy, The Mole, The Fox and the Horse by Charlie Mackesy
The Most Magnificent Thing by Ashley Spires
My Very Favorite Book in the Whole Wide World by Malcolm Mitchell; illus. Michael Robertson
The One Thing You'd Save by Linda Sue Park; illus. Robert Sae-Heng
The Rock From the Sky by Jon Klassen

Write to Read: Quickwriting

Writing Tip

Quickwrite is a useful strategy before, while, or after you listen to a teacher read aloud a picture book, novel, poem, or nonfiction selection. You can respond personally to the text by recording thoughts and opinions about the text, or perhaps in response to a question posed by the teacher.

1. You are invited to quickwrite on a topic or question assigned by your teacher or chosen on your own. Here are some questions that might inspire quickwrites:

   - What is your earliest memory?
   - What will you be doing this evening?
   - What books would be on the bookshelf of your life?
   - What does the word *kindness* mean to you?
   - What do you see outside your window?
   - What do you expect your future to be like?
   - What superhero power do you wish you had?
   - What is your special talent?

2. On a signal, write freely, transferring brain activity to the page.
3. Work in pairs to share your quickwrite. You can read your quickwrite aloud or partners can read each other's work silently. Offer questions or suggestions for the person to extend their work. What information might need to be added to the piece?
4. Work independently for another five to seven minutes to add to your quickwrite piece.

Let's Go Further: One Word

Often a word can lead to a story. For example, quickwrites could be prompted by words like *stitches, accident, vacation, surprise, lost, hiking, family, embarrassment,* etc. Choose a word that appears in the title of the book you are reading, on the first page of a novel, or displayed on the walls of your classroom. You can use this single word as inspiration for a quickwrite activity.

Quizzes

A quiz asks a series of questions used to test someone's knowledge about a topic.

Read to Write: Nonfiction Picture Books on Identity

Fry Bread: A Native American Family Story by Kevin Noble Maillard; illus. Juana Martinez-Neal

Sharing Our Truths (Tapwe) by Henry Beaver and Mindy Willet with Eileen Beaver; photographs by Tessa Macintosh

Turtle Island: The Story of North America's First People by Eldon Yellow-horn and Kathy Lowinger

The Water Walker by Joanne Robertson

Write to Read: Creating a Quiz

Writing Tip

Developing a quiz can be done independently, but when you do it as a group, it is a talk task that promotes work with others.

1. Review the types of questions that could be asked in a quiz:

   True/False: provides a statement which could be true or false
   Multiple Choice: offers three (or four) answers to choose from
   Fill in the Blank: presents a statement with a blank space to insert a word related to the topic

2. Work alone or with a partner to prepare a fact quiz on an inquiry topic. You cam use a picture book on a topic in Science or Social Studies to prepare your quiz. Alternatively, an article, report, or nonfiction text could be a source for testing someone's knowledge about what they have read.

3. The questions you create should focus on just the facts about a topic. Your quiz should include all three types of questions.

4. Once you have prepared 10 to 12 questions, exchange quizzes with others and work independently to answer each other's questions. You can, if you wish, score each other's answers.

Let's Go Further: The Class Quiz

The class is divided into small groups of two or three to prepare a quiz connected to a curriculum area that has been explored in the class: e.g., Animal Habitats (Science); The Election Process (Social Studies); The Human Body (Health). Each group can contribute questions for the teacher to choose and present to the whole class.

Quotations

Quotations are inspirational words that offer an authoritative voice to support an idea or issue.

Read to Write: Collections of Inspirational Quotations

A Gift of Days: The Greatest Words to Live By edited by Stephen Alcorn
Pete the Cat's Groovy Guide to Life by Kimberley and James Dean
365 Days of Wonder: Mr. Browne's Precepts edited by R.J. Palacio
The Ultimate Book of Inspiring Quotes for Kids by Michael Stutman and
   Kevin Conklin
Zen Pencils: Inspirational Quotes for Kids by Gavin Aung Than

In the novel *Wonder* by R.J. Palacio, Auggie Pullman's classroom teacher, Mr. Browne, inspires his students by presenting precepts to engage and enlighten them. Beyond that, R.J. Palacio's book *365 Days of Wonder* features a memorable quotation about courage, friendship, love, or kindness for every day of the year. Consider quotations or precepts that can be presented into the classroom as a daily ritual.

Write to Read: Responding to and Researching Quotations

Writing Tip

Consider some quotations that appear as posters around your school. Is there a quotation or saying that is often repeated within your family? For example, *Don't expect and you won't be disappointed. If you want something done, do it yourself.* In groups of three or four, prepare a list of familiar quotations that offer advice or philosophies for others to consider.

1. Choose one quotation from the Writers on Writing handout that interests you.
2. Prepare a written response by considering these questions:

   - What does this quotation mean to you?
   - Why did you choose this particular quotation?
   - What experiences/connections does this quotation remind you of?
   - How is this statement inspirational for reflecting on the writing process?

3. Meet in groups of four or five to share your responses to the quotations. Which was the most popular choice of quotation?

Let's Go Further: Inspirational Quotations

Work alone or with a partner to choose a topic that interests you: e.g., kindness, friendship, education, peace, making a difference, etc. Find at least five quotations on the internet to share with others. Choose your favorite quotation to be displayed on a banner, poster, or class blog to share with families and others in the community. Get together with other students and contribute an image slide of a quotation to create a class slide show. Inspirational quotations can be presented in the classroom as a daily ritual event.

Reading Response Journals

The reading response journal is a vehicle for you to communicate your thoughts and feelings about texts you are exposed to.

Write to Read: Keeping a Reading Response Journal

Use your reading response journal to record your thoughts about what you read. You can write whatever you wish, but keep in mind these tips:

1. It is important that your entries do not always—or only—retell the story. To become more reflective of your reading, consider using reading strategies:

   - asking questions
   - making connections to your life; making connections to other books
   - making predictions
   - highlighting vocabulary
   - creating illustrations, offering opinions, and sharing what you wondered about as you read.

2. Here are some examples of prompts that could inspire you to think about what you read:

   What did you enjoy (or not enjoy) about what you read?
   What, if anything, puzzled you as you read?
   How do you feel about the way the author presented the story?
   What did you wonder about as you read?
   On a scale of 1 to 10, how would you rate this book? Explain.
   What might you tell others about what you have read?

   See the Reading Response Journals: Journal Prompts for a full list of prompts.

Read to Write: Responding to Responses

As an audience for someone's journal entries you can

- question things you don't understand or the responder has not clarified
- ask for more information on a particular interpretation
- pose questions that involve rethinking or rereading
- share your own experiences as a reader or writer
- recommend other titles or genres of books
- value responses and acknowledge the responder's thoughts and feelings

Let's Go Further: Literature Circles

A literature circle is a small group of students reading the same book who meet to discuss, react, and share their responses to it. When coming to a Literature Circle meeting, bring your *literature log* (a reading response journal for the book you are all reading) and be prepared to share your thinking and use your notes to stimulate discussion with other group members.

Writing Tips

- See the Journal Prompts handout for a more extensive list of prompts to inspire you to respond to what you read.
- Sharing journal entries with others can begin a dialogue, as the reader of your journal points out connections they had to the shared thoughts, and expresses their own opinions and viewpoints about what you have offered. An exchange of journals can lead to either oral or written responses on sticky notes or in the journal, as if having a dialogue.

Recipes

Recipes provide instructions on how to prepare a food item or a favorite meal.

Read to Write: Cookbook Search

Collect cookbooks from your home and/or the library. In groups, share the cookbooks and discuss what makes the book appealing. How clearly is the recipe information presented? What headings are used to organize instructions? How are illustrations, photographs used?

Write to Read: Let's Eat!

Writing Tips
- You and your classmates can gather recipes in a class book, in print or digitally, for others to read and try.
- The picture book *Pizza! A Slice of History* by Greg Pizzoli tells about the history and appeal of this popular food. What's your favorite pizza recipe?

1. Choose a food item you enjoy eating and have made before or watched someone else make.
2. Without referring to a print recipe, create step by step instructions that would help others prepare this dish. This checklist might help you to write your recipe:

   ☐ List ingredients
   ☐ Include quantities for all ingredients
   ☐ Note equipment that might be needed
   ☐ Write the steps, in order, to make this dish. Are the steps numbered?
   ☐ Offer suggestions or cooking tips to make this a successful recipe for others to follow

3. For more practice, you can write a recipe for a favorite meal you have prepared. These recipes can be illustrated.
4. With classmates, gather recipes in a class book, in print or digital, for others to read.

Let's Go Further: Beyond Cooking

The recipe format can be used to create instructions for a non-food item. You can share

- a recipe for being a good friend
- a recipe for choosing a good pet
- a recipe for kindness
- a recipe for world peace
- a recipe for being a hero, athlete, or celebrity

Recounts

A recount is the retelling or recounting of an event or experience.

Read to Write: Picture Book Recounts

> *Alexander and the Terrible, Horrible, No Good, Very Bad Day* by Judith Viorst; illus. Ray Cruz
> *The Relatives Came* by Cynthia Rylant; illus. Stephen Gammell
> *Last Stop on Market Street* by Matt de la Peña; illus. Christian Robinson
> *Owl Moon* by Jane Yolen; illus. John Schoenherr

Write to Read: Recount from Your Life

Writing Tip
Good writers consider their readers. Use the Recount Checklist handout to make sure your recount includes information your readers will need and has the effect on your readers you want.

1. Think about a story from your life for one of these titles:

   - My Trip to…
   - A Family Celebration
   - The First Time I…
   - My Scariest Moment

   - Lost!
   - Stitches/Scars
   - How Embarrassing!
   - The Sleepover

2. Consider what experience to tell about; what your reader will need to know early in the text; events and the order they will occur; how you will let your readers know the order of events; other information that might be useful to include; how to conclude your recount.
3. To prepare to write, work with one or two classmates to tell your story before writing.
4. These points can help you consider writing a recount successfully. Recounts

   - are written in chronological order
   - are written in first person
   - are written in the past tense
   - use time/sequencing words and phrases

Let's Go Further: Recount as a Graphic Story

Transform your recount into a graphic story by creating verbal text and illustrations to tell the beginning, middle, and end of your story. The comic strip format can help you show

- Who: character(s) shown in each panel
- When: captions for the sequence of events
- What: each panel shows what happened
- Where: the setting can vary between panels

Reviews

A review can help us decide whether we are interested in reading a book, seeing a movie or show, or listening to music.

Read to Write: Investigating a Book Review

Read a book review in a newspaper or magazine or find a review online of a favorite book that you have read. In some cases, you may find more than one review of a book and these opinions might be similar or different. Do you agree or disagree with the reviewer's opinion?

Write to Read: Writing a Book Review

1. Select a book you have recently read, either one you enjoyed or one you didn't find appealing.
2. In point form, briefly list the main story line or content, telling about the characters, setting, and problem of the book. List two or three convincing reasons why others should or should not read the book.
3. Prepare a draft of the review.

   - Write a lead sentence to capture the readers' attention and state the main idea of the piece.
   - Describe three or four specific events, relationships, or conversations that would help readers understand what has happened in the book.
   - Consider quoting a passage from the book to support your views.
   - Give your opinions of how the author told the story (e.g., use of language, style, etc.)
   - Conclude the review with a recommendation to read the book or not.

4. Work in pairs or small groups and exchange reviews. You can further share your opinions by discussing each of the books. Discussion might lead you to revisit your review to add details.
5. Extend your book review experience by writing a review of something other than a book: TV show, movie, play, concert, recital, YouTube video, etc.

Let's Go Further: Book Talk

You can use your reviews to prepare a short book talk for the class. A book talk is an oral book report where you share your views of the book and inspire others to read the book.

Writing Tip

In some cases, you may find more than one review of a book in a newspaper or magazine, or online. The opinions might be similar or different. Do you agree or disagree with the reviewer's opinion?

Rules

Rules are needed to play sports or games. Safety rules ensure order and prevent injury.

Read to Write: *Rules* by Cynthia Lord

This novel tells the story of a girl trying care for a brother with autism. Each chapter begins with a rule to help her brother cope and not embarrass himself; e.g., *Keep our pants on in public.*

Write to Read: The Rules of the Game

Writing Tip
To prepare for writing rules for a game, work with two friends and orally prepare a list of instructions that need to be followed to play the game effectively.

1. Work in pairs and decide on a game you are both familiar with. It can be a sport, a game played on the playground or in gym class, a board game like chess or checkers, etc.
2. With your partner, develop a list of instructions needed to play the game. In addition to what a player does, consider number of players; how a winner is determined, if there is a winner; what is allowed in game play; what is not allowed in game play; and penalties if rules are broken.
3. Working independently, write your rules in point form. Review your notes and consider what has been omitted and what is unnecessary. Make sure the instructions are in order.
4. Write a first draft of your game rules. Think about including time-order words for sequencing instructions (e.g., *First, Next, Then*). Consider adding tips on how to successfully play.
5. Exchange lists with your partner. If directions are clearly written, neither of you should have problems playing the game from the written rules. Is some information missing from your rules? How might you edit one or more rules to explain directions clearly?

Let's Go Further: Safety Rules

Rules can keep things safe and orderly. Working alone or in pairs, write five or more safety rules for one of the following situations:

- at school (the playground, the halls, in class, in the cafeteria)
- at the local swimming pool or recreation centre
- for bicycle riding
- to prevent fires
- for young children going out for Halloween

Share your list of rules with two or three classmates. Were the rules presented clearly? Which rules are easy to follow? Which are the most challenging to follow?

Scripts for Readers Theatre

A script tells a story through the speech of characters in a play. In Readers Theatre, a script is developed from material not initially written for performance.

Read to Write: Novel to Script

Novels are useful sources for Readers Theatre scripts. Investigate scenes from a favorite novel you think might be dramatized for an audience. The scene should be no more than two pages and should feature conversations involving one or more characters. How would you transform this scene into a script?

Write to Read: Writing a Readers Theatre Script

Writing Tip
When developing Readers Theatre scripts, you need to make decisions about the role of a narrator (or more than one narrator) as well as the dialogue spoken by different characters.

1. When choosing text from a novel to develop a Readers Theatre script, look for text that includes dialogue. Other text sources:

   - Photograph or illustration featuring at least two characters: write the conversation the characters might be having.
   - Graphic text: The speech bubbles can be written as script.
   - Improvise an interview (with a story character, author, celebrity, or expert).
   - A fable: designate lines to be read by narrator and characters.
   - Transcription from recorded oral conversation.

2. Review script format before writing your script. Dialogue follows *Narrator* or the name of the character speaking it and a colon; each change in who is speaking starts a new line. Here is an example of a Readers Theatre script developed from a passage from the novel *Ground Zero* by Alan Gratz:

   Narrator: A white Port Authority policewoman with her hair in a brown ponytail pointed the boys toward the staircase.
   Richard: Wait, doesn't this go to the basement? Why can't we just go outside?
   Policewoman: We can't take you through the lobby. It's too full of injured people. And it's dangerous right outside the building.
   Narrator: Brandon knew why. Outside through the window he could still hear what sounded like pebbles and stones raining down on the concrete plaza.

Let's Go Further: Dramatizing Your Readers Theatre Script

An essential extension of writing scripts is to read your writing out loud. Memorizing lines is not important unless your script is being performed for an audience. As a group, choose a script, assign roles, and rehearse, considering

- Will we stand or sit to present the scene?
- What actions or gestures will we use?
- How will we use voice to convey meaning and emotions?
- How will rehearsal help us become familiar with our parts?
- How do we imagine the script to be presented in a theatre?

Social Media

Social media give users quick electronic communication of content through virtual networks: e.g., blogs, email, texting, social networks (Twitter, Instagram, TikTok, etc.)

Read to Write: Novels Using Social Media Forms

36 Questions that Changed My Mind About You by Vicki Grant
This is So Awkward by Lisa Greenwald
TTYL by Lauren Myracle (series: Internet Girls)

Do you find that your use of social media is like that shown in the book?

Write to Read: Text Talk

1. Have an email or text conversation with a partner. The following question prompts can be used to begin the conversation:

   - What are you reading these days?
   - What do you think about homework?
   - What's the most interesting thing you did this week?
   - What does your bedroom look like?
   - Do you think you spend too much time on social media?
   - What do you think you learn by playing video games?

2. Now share your digital conversation by reading it aloud to another pair.

Let's Go Further Social Media in Role

Use your familiarity and expertise with social media to write in role using a virtual network. You can take the perspective of a character from a novel, a real person, or even an animal to send messages to others. For example: What message might send Mahmoud send to his family in Alan Gratz's *Refugee*? What would an Instagram page look like for Wimpy Kid in the series by Jeff Kinney? What text messages would the animals exchange in *The One and Only Ivan* by Katherine Applegate?

Writing Tip

You need to be aware that what you post on social media may be available online forever. If you don't want family members, teachers, or even future employers to see something, it shouldn't be online.

Surveys

Surveys are interviews to get people's opinions about a topic or issue.

Read to Write: Writing Survey

1.	I read a novel every day.	YES	NO
2.	I enjoy writing poetry.	YES	NO
3.	I prefer to write a) information b) stories c) recounts c) other: _____		
4.	I choose to write without teacher suggestions.	OFTEN SOMETIMES NEVER	
5.	I enjoy sharing my writing with others to read.	OFTEN SOMETIMES NEVER	
6.	Most of my writing is done on the computer.	YES	NO

Write to Read: Creating a Survey

Writing Tip

Survey-taking can be oral. Once you have prepared your questions, you can conduct an interview with at least eight people answering. The interviewer has the task of recording answers to questions they ask the interviewees.

1. Working alone or with a partner, choose a topic: e.g., Video Games, Homework, Favorites.
2. Prepare a list of at least 6 questions about your topic. Surveys might include the following kinds of questions:

   - Yes/No
   - Multiple-choice
   - Fill-in-the-bank
   - Open-ended
   - Rating scale: e.g., 1 to 5; Never/Sometimes/Often

3. Exchange surveys with a partner (or another group if you are working in pairs) to take.
4. Survey-taking can be oral. You can interview and record answers from at least 8 people.
5. Present the results of your survey or questionnaire as a graph to summarize information learned.

Let's Go Further: Assumption Guides

An assumption guide is designed to help you examine what people think or feel about a particular issue (e.g., bullying, gender equity, physical and mental challenges, etc.). To create an assumption guide, prepare a list of statements to arouse opinions, beliefs, or attitudes about the topic. Based on your experiences and assumptions, you accept statements as true or false.

Thank-You Messages

Thank-you messages are a form of personal writing that demonstrate gratitude for a gift, as an acknowledgment of a donation, or as an appreciation for a favor or kindness.

Read to Write: *Thank You, Mr. Falker* by Patricia Polacco

In this picture book, the author pays tribute to the teacher who taught her to read. How does the author take her thank-you beyond a note to an authentic piece of writing for an audience?

Write to Read: Writing Thank-You Notes

1. Decide what you would like to thank someone for. It can be a personal message to someone you know, or to show gratitude to someone who has put forth a special effort for the community.
2. Use the following guide to help extend a thank-you message beyond a short note to make it more meaningful.

   - Who will be receiving this message (salutation)?
   - Why is the note being written?
   - What details can you add? For example, telling how the gift will be used, or your opinion of the gift or gesture.
   - What anecdote or personal greeting might you add?
   - What words will you use to sign off the message?

3. You can send your thank-you message as a letter, email message, or illustrated greeting card.

Let's Go Further: Fictional Thank-You Note

Write a fictional thank-you note from a story or novel character's point of view. What might Goldilocks say to the Three Bears? What note might Auggie Pullman send to his teacher Mr. Browne in *Wonder* by R.J. Palacio?

Thinking Stems

Thinking stems, or prompts, invite you to respond in writing to a story, poem, article, or topic. Sample stems include *I like…; I learned…; I predict…; I'm puzzled by…; I'm reminded of…; I wonder…,* etc.

Read to Write: *Morris Micklewhite and the Tangerine Dress* by Christine Baldacchino, illustrated by Isabelle Malenfant

Here are some student responses to a read-aloud of this book about a young boy who enjoys wearing a dress during play time, even though he is teased by others in his class:

I feel… *happy that Morris stuck up for himself.*
I remember… *another book called* You're Mean, Lily Jean *about a girl who was excluded.*
I wonder… *what I would do if I was in Morris's class.*

Write to Read: Using Thinking Stems to Respond to Reading

Writing Tip

Using thinking stems is a meaningful strategy to implement when you listen to something being read aloud by the teacher. However, thinking stems can also be used when you independently read poems, nonfiction selections, or novels.

1. After listening to a read-aloud, as a class choose three specific prompts to focus on and complete; for example:

   I feel…
   I like…
   I wonder…

2. Once you have completed your responses, meet in groups of three or four to share your responses. The whole class can have a discussion about the text where different views are shared.
3. Now choose from the list of Thinking Stems Sample Prompts to write about something you've read independently; e.g., a poem, a novel, a nonfiction selection.

Let's Go Further: Thinking Stems Beyond Reading

Thinking stems can be used to share responses in a variety of contexts, such as

- viewing a film
- watching a YouTube video
- watching an episode on TV or streaming
- reading or listening to news event
- having a conversation with a friend or friends
- following a class discussion

Titles

Titles help readers choose what to read, watch, or listen to.

Read to Write: Judging a Book by Its Title

Prepare a list of five favorite titles for each of these categories: Picture Books, Novels, Films, Songs. Keep in mind that a good title

- catches the reader's attention with specific word choices
- inspires readers to wonder what the text will be about
- is often short
- has all important words capitalized: first word, last word, nouns, verbs, adjectives
- has prepositions (e.g., *in, of, at*) and articles (*a, an, the*) not capitalized
- can be a line of text excerpted from the content

Once completed, meet in groups of two or three to share choices. Discuss what makes the title appealing.

Write to Read: Inspired by a Title

Writing Tip

Using punctuation correctly is an important part of writing titles. The first word is always a capital letter. Most words written in a title should begin with a capital letter, especially names of people, places, and things.

1. Find two or three books whose stories you are not familiar with.
2. Which title sparks ideas for your own writing? For example, what story might you consider for the following picture book titles?

   The Day War Came by Nicola Davies
   Finding Kindness by Deborah Underwood
   The Most Magnificent Thing by Ashley Spires
   The Promise by Margie Wolfe and Pnina Bat Zvi
   Shh! We Have a Plan by Chris Haughton

3. Write your own story based on the title.

Let's Go Further: Designing a Title Page

Create a title page for a story you have written or a report you have completed. Consider:

- How will the title page grab a reader's attention?
- What illustration or design will be included on the page?
- How will words and illustrations be formatted on the page?
- Will there be a border design?
- What font(s) will be used?
- How will your name be featured?

Transcriptions

A transcription is a written record of oral talk: a conversation, an interview, a drama improvisation, etc.

Read to Write: Nonfiction Books

There are nonfiction books that are presented as transcriptions of oral speech. In some cases students told stories connected to an issue and then wrote them down; for others, the author interviewed and recorded student voices that were later transcribed.

> *Kids Speak out About Immigration* by Chris Schwab
> *Three Wishes: Palestinian and Israeli Children Speak* by Deborah Ellis
> *We Are Their Voice: Young People Respond to the Holocaust* by Kathy Kacer
> *What Does Hate Look Like?* by Corinne Promislow, Sameea Jimenez, Larry Swartz

Write to Read: Transcribing Talk

Writing Tip
To determine how clear your transcript is, exchange your writing with another pair to read aloud. Did the transcription seem like a real conversation? Was the language clear? Were there any gaps in the conversation?

For this activity, you will work in pairs to record talk that can be transcribed.

1. Choose an issue or topic to discuss: e.g., *Money brings happiness; Athletes deserve to get as high a fee as possible; Once a bully, always a bully; Competition is a good thing; Pink is for girls/blue is for boys.*
2. Have a recording device or app ready.
3. Have a short conversation (5 minutes) with both of you having a chance to speak.
4. Play back and listen to the whole conversation. Decide which parts of the talk you would like to write out.
5. Write what you hear, stopping and starting the recording as much as you need to get the words written. The completed transcript will look like a script, giving the name of the speaker and then the words they said:

Joshua: Maybe a bully is a bully because someone has bullied them.
Ayla: You have a good point there, but I think it's important to confront bullies. I know it's hard to do but I think someone who is bullied needs to let the bully know how they feel.

Let's Go Further: Transcribing Group Talk

Record and transcribe a group talk. Participants need to be told in advance that their conversations will be recorded. Some suggestions for topics:

- solving a math problem
- trying to analyze a poem
- a literature circle discussion
- playing a game
- a lunch-time conversation
- a discussion about a hot topic issue
- an imaginary interview; e.g., a story character, celebrity, or historical figure

Urban Tales

Urban tales are presented as stories that have been passed down over the years. The more the story is retold, the more it might change.

Read to Write: "The Hook"

As urban tales are told and retold, sometimes they are recorded. "The Hook" is an urban tale that originated in the 1950s and has been retold in a number of versions in print and movies. Sometimes called "The Claw," it recounts the story of a murderer with a pirate-hook in place of a hand. In many written and oral versions the killer appears as a faceless man who wears a raincoat to disguise his features. You can find and read versions of this story on the internet. How do the details of the story differ? How has the story changed over time?

Write to Read: Collaborative Storytelling

Writing Tip
You can rewrite the story in the first-person voice. In this way you can imagine that you were a participant or eyewitness to the tale.

1. In a small group of four or five, sit in a circle.
2. As a group, choose an opening line to start the story; e.g., *It was a dark and stormy night*; *Everybody was warned, but nobody listened*; *Everything changed when the stranger came to town*; etc.
3. One person is designated to start the story with the opening line and another sentence or two to continue the narrative.
4. After one minute, the person to the right of the story starter continues the story.
5. The storytelling continues around the circle, with each person given one minute to add to the story, until the story has travelled the circle two or three times and a satisfying ending to the story is told.

Let's Go Further: Writing an Urban Tale

Choose one of the urban tale stories the group invented and write it as an urban tale. Compare your writing with that of another group member who chose the same story. How are your stories different? How do you account for the differences?

Voice

Voice is at the heart of writing. When we read good writing we "hear" the sound of another human talking to you.

Read to Write: Voice 1–2–3

In fiction, an author uses one of three voices:

- First person uses the pronoun "I" or "we"
- Second person uses the pronoun "you" (not commonly used in fiction)
- Third person uses the pronouns "he," "she," and "they"

Gather a number of novels or picture books from the classroom or school library. Consider whether the author has used first person, second person, or third person voice. Why do you think the choice of voice was made?

Write to Read: Capturing Voice

1. Select an excerpt from fiction you have enjoyed reading that is written in the third person. This piece should be about half a page in length (perhaps the opening to the novel).
2. Transform the excerpt into the first person by using the pronoun "I." The story becomes your own as you become the main character.
3. Feel free to add words, describe feelings, and use vivid verbs to put the passage in your own voice.

Let's Go Further: Keeping a Log of Voice Writing

Over a week-long period of independent reading, keep a record of words, phrases, sentences, or dialogue from books or nonfiction that you think are unique, are original, or sound "like talk." Collect writing that makes you go "ahhh"—a reaction most likely to the author's voice.

You can share your log entries with others in your class and explain your choices of voice writing that puts personality on paper.

Writing Tip

An essential tip for capturing voice in your writing is to sound like yourself. Use vocabulary and sentence types that you use in your everyday speech.

Word Games

Games with words can enrich your understanding of spelling patterns and vocabulary choices for your writing.

Read to Write: What's the Pattern?

Choose ten to twelve words from any book you are reading. Arrange the words into three columns, with each focusing on a single pattern. For example, with weather words—*rain, storm, raindrops, sleet, thunder, clouds, ice, icy, rainy, rainbow, precipitation, puddles, blizzard, tornado*—you could put *raindrops, rainbow,* and *rainy* together since they contain the word *rain*; you could put *raindrops, clouds,* and *puddles* together since they are plural words; *ice, clouds, sleet, storm, rain* are one-syllable words.

Write to Read: Games with Words

Word Scramble
Players take a long word (e.g., *concentration, Tyrannosaurus, neighborhood, Global Warming*) and take 3 minutes to list many new words of three letters or more that can be made from the letters in the word. Note: a letter can be used only as many times as it appears in the word.

Word Race
Teams of two or three are challenged to compile a list of as many words as possible within a time limit. Choose a pattern for the words:

- end with the suffix *–tion*
- end with the suffix *–ture*
- include the letter *x*
- double consonants
- have 4 syllables
- have 3 different vowels

When time is up, teams compare lists.

Let's Go Further: Creating a Word Puzzle

Work alone or with a partner to create a word puzzle for others to solve:

- a crossword puzzle with short definition
- a word searches on a theme or topic
- matching words in Column A with definitions in Column B
- unscrambling letters to form a word
- fill in the blanks with missing letters; e.g. add vowels; add consonants; add vowels or consonants

Writing Tip
For these activities, it is important that words be spelled correctly. You can check with friends and/or use the dictionary to spell check words that might not be familiar to you.

Word Power

Writing cannot happen without words. The more words you know, the more you can choose for your writing and the deeper your understanding of the power of the word.

Read to Write: *The Word Collector* by Peter H. Reynolds

Jerome delights in filling scrapbooks with words that he hears, sees, and reads. Reynolds presents an invitation to readers of all ages to pay attention (and collect) words that are short, that are sweet, that puzzle and mystify; words that are marvelous to say; words to carry in our language backpacks to take out as needed when reading, writing, and conversing.

Write to Read: Ways to Increase Your Word Power

Writing Tip

Working collaboratively with one or two friends can add power to activities. When brainstorming with others, you and your group can offer suggestions for your vocabulary lists, as well as help each other with checking that words are spelled correctly.

1. What's in a Name?
   Brainstorm up to ten items for one of the following categories:

   - a name for a pet hamster
   - picture book titles
   - favorite movies
   - city names of more than three syllables
   - authors

   Names must be spelled and capitalized correctly.

2. Alphabet List
   Write the letters of the alphabet in a vertical column. Choose one of the topics below and find a word (or two) that fits for each letter of the alphabet:

   - things we write
   - athletes
   - authors
   - countries
   - fruits and vegetables
   - zoo animals

3. Word Web
   Choose a root word from this list: *cent, snow, land, form, ant*. Write the root word at the centre and create a word web of as many words you can that contain that root word.

Let's Go Further: Becoming a Word Collector

- Use sticky notes to identify text pages where interesting or unfamiliar words appear
- Post interesting words on sticky notes on a classroom bulletin board entitled *We Collect Words*
- Go on a word hunt for words that fit a pattern
- Participate in a Word of the Day program. When designated, you present a new word you discovered in your reading or in a word-of-the-day app.

Writing in Role

Writing in role is writing from a character's perspective in a familiar format such as a letter, email, diary, or text. For drama, writing in role can also be used for monologues (first-person speech by a character), interviews (e.g., media interviews, talk-shows, etc.), or improvisation (e.g., where a character retells their story).

Write to Read: The Bully, The Bullied, The Bystander

1. Working in groups of three or four, imagine that you are taking part in a documentary to help young people understand the various perspectives involved in bullying. Within the documentary there will be interviews with people have bullied, have been bullied, and have witnessed bullying behavior.
2. To prepare for the documentary, write a recount from one of the perspectives. Your recount will tell a story from the point of view of the bully, the bullied, or the bystander about an incident that happened at school. Who was involved? How did the incident get started? What dialogue was heard? How did the characters behave? React? How did the incident end?

Read to Write: Reading Your Writing

Your writing can be used for drama exploration in which each group member assumes assume the role of a character. You can improvise from your writing:

- The Bully and the Bullied have a conversation
- The Bully and the Bystander have a conversation
- The Bullied and the Bystander have a conversation

Let's Go Further: Writing a Letter in Role

Write a letter from one character to another. What might you say to have the other person reflect on the bullying incident? How will you move forward (or not) from the incident?

Let's Go Further: Using Technology in Role

Work with a partner or in a small group and exchange text messages or e-mails in role. You can write as characters from the same novel or as characters from different novels. Your messages might retell events, reveal problems, and/or raise questions. Take about 10 minutes to create a text message exchange. Then, as a follow-up, read aloud the text messages as dialogue script, with each of you taking on a role. The text message dialogue can be transformed into a script to be rehearsed and presented.

Writing Tip

Writing in role is in the first person, using the pronoun "I." You are pretending to be someone else, but are challenged to make the writing as authentic as possible by not only describing what happens to a character but also conveying that character's feelings as they experience problems and discuss relationships.

Xpert Writing

Xpert writing can be lists of facts about a topic (to inform), can give rules or instructions (to explain), and/or can tell a story about how the writer became an expert on the topic (to narrate).

Read to Write: Animal Xperts

Many writers of nonfiction are experts in the topics they present. They might have a personal interest or knowledge about a topic or issue but they also do extensive research to share information with others. The following picture book titles confirm that the authors are experts about animals:

> *Honeybee: The Busy Life of Apis Mellifera* by Candace Fleming; illus. Eric Rohmann
> *Bat Citizens: Defending the Ninjas of the Night* by Rob Laidlaw
> *Loon* by Susan Vande Griek; illus. Karen Reczuch
> *The Tragic Tale of the Great Auk* by Jan Thornhill

Write to Read: Write as an Xpert

Writing Tip

After writing as an expert, return to your original piece. Continue writing and adding information that helps to prove that you are an expert on the topic. Consider researching your topic through print or digital texts. What additional information might you add to your expert piece? Are there descriptive details you might add to your writing?

1. List three things that you feel you know a lot about: e.g., a game, a sport, a hobby, a craft, an animal, a country, etc.
2. Review your list and put an asterisk (*) beside one you think you might be an expert on.
3. Prepare a quickwrite on your topic of choice. See how much information you can get down by writing continuously for five or six minutes.
4. Work in pairs to share your pieces. Each of you can ask questions to help gather more information about a topic from other writer.

Let's Go Further: Everything You Wanted to Know About…

You can revise and edit your xpert piece in one of the following ways:

- Write a magazine or newspaper article
- Create a brochure that includes information (and pictures) about the topic
- Share information in graphic text format
- Write a fictitious letter to apply for a job that uses your expertise
- Write in question and answer format, as if being interviewed by a reporter

Yarns

A yarn is a humorous tale of made-up events.

Read to Write: Types of Tales

When you hear the words *tall tale* or *believe-it-or-not story*, what kind of stories come to mind? You can investigate examples of stories known as yarns that can have been knitted together from real and made-up facts.

Write to Read: Writing a Yarn

Writing Tip
Make your yarn tale as believable as possible by considering the features of narrative writing, voice, and realistic details.

1. Meet with two or three classmates. Together, choose any three items from the Tic-Tac-Toe Chart handout that appear in a straight line, vertically, horizontally, or diagonally.
2. Use the three chosen phrases to invent a humorous story that could be true.
3. Based on your oral storytelling, work independently to write a yarn story. Use the features of narrative writing to organize your story:

   - The beginning introduces the main characters and their problem.
   - The middle tells what the main characters did and what happens.
   - The conclusion tells how the main characters solve their problem and how the story ends.

4. Meet in pairs to exchange yarn stories. Before sharing your written stories, each partner tells their story. Then read your partner's story to determine how the oral story and written story compare.

Let's Go Further: Unbelievable!

These titles might inspire you to write more humorous yarn tales:

- The Day My Dog Saved the Day
- He Shoots! He Scores... 10 times!
- How Uncle Pete Got His Name in the Guinness Book of Records
- The Butterfly Infestation
- Alien Invasion
- If At First You Don't Succeed, Try, Try Again.
- Ding, Dong, the Robot's Dead!

Zodiac

The constellation zodiac is made up of twelve signs named for stellar constellations and based on when in the year you were born. By charting the signs of the zodiac in horoscopes, astrologists claim to be able to read character and foretell the future.

Read to Write: What's Your Sign?

Using the Zodiac Charts handout, identify your sign of the constellation zodiac. Search the internet for character descriptions associated with your sign and record three or four items you think best apply to you. Meet in groups of three or four to share information you have learned about your zodiac sign. How accurate is the description for each student?

Write to Read: Writing Horoscopes

Writing Tip
The dictionary defines zodiac as imaginary. There are many strong believers in astrology, but some would argue that astrology is not a real science. Share your opinions of horoscopes with others. Do the horoscopes you have written seem believable?

1. Use the internet to find and read the daily horoscope for your constellation zodiac sign.
2. Meet in groups of three or four, making sure you all have different horoscopes. Discuss:

   - What opinion(s) does each horoscope share?
   - How did you feel about reading your horoscope? Did you like it? If not, why not?
   - Are the predictions suitable for people of all ages?
   - What questions come to mind about the horoscope?

3. Write an imaginary horoscope for tomorrow. Present three or four predictions for those born under your sign. You can work independently or with a partner who has the same sign as you. Your challenge is to write believable and relevant predictions.
4. The next day, meet again and discuss how accurate the horoscope predictions you found were. Follow up the day after that to see how accurate your own predictions were.

Let's Go Further: Exploring the Chinese Zodiac

The Chinese zodiac, which is also followed in other Asian countries, features a cycle of twelve animal signs that represent a year each and appear in this order: Rat, Ox, Tiger, Rabbit, Dragon, Snake, Horse, Sheep, Monkey, Rooster, Dog, and Pig. Use the Zodiac Charts handout to identify your animal; search the internet to find and read the description of your Chinese zodiac sign. Is the description accurate or not? How like the Chinese zodiac animal are you? What information might you change in this description? What might you add?

Teacher Resources

Functions of Writing

Writing to Explain

Announcements

Lesson on page 17.

An announcement is a public declaration of an event, or something that has happened or will be happening. Whether a written announcement is displayed on a bulletin board or presented in a newsletter or classroom blog, it should answer the questions *Who? What? Where? When? Why?* and *How?* in order to effectively communicate information to an audience.

Teaching Tip

Announcements are written with an audience in mind. Sometimes, the audience is anonymous (e.g., announcing a bake sale in the community); at other times the announcement is written with a specific audience in mind (the class or school community). Announcements can be put on display on a bulletin board or presented orally for others to listen to. To determine how successful students were at preparing an announcement, have them practice reading the announcement out loud.

Brochures

Lesson on page 22.

Brochures are a type of advertising primarily used to inform others about a person, place, or thing. A brochure is most used as a marketing tool to promote a product, a service, or a place of interest to visit. Many companies and health organizations create brochures, since they are an effective and efficient way to present essential information to customers or members of the public about the benefits the organization can offer.

Characterizations

Lesson on page 23.

Characterizations are vivid portraits of a character. A writer makes characters come alive by telling what they look like, what they wear, how they speak, and what other characters say about them. Writing characterizations can help students practice descriptive writing and consider the use of details and information that paint a clear picture of a character's physical description, personality, and behaviors.

Teaching Tips

- As students read novels, they will encounter vivid descriptions of characters. Usually this information is presented in the early pages of the story so the reader has a clear picture of the character. Provide sticky notes for students to mark interesting descriptive passages where the author paints a vivid description of a story character. These excerpts can be displayed in the class and used as mentor texts for description as students consider the author's choice of words, use of similes, and clarity of detail.
- Tell students to imagine that a person has gone missing and needs to be found. A wanted poster will be displayed in the community with details that provide a detailed character description of that person/creature. An illustration could be featured in the poster. The wanted poster could be used to describe one of the following:

  - a wizard
  - a monster
  - an alien creature
  - a burglar

  - a pirate
  - a robot

Definitions

Lesson on page 27.

A definition is a statement of the meaning of a word. Dictionaries are concerned with denotation, or the exact meaning of a word. Writers often need to choose a word because of its particular associations or implications. By having students take on the role of dictionary editors, they can choose vocabulary they think is most relevant to define a concept.

Teaching Tip

Implement a shared writing activity to arrive at a class definition of a word. Record each suggestion offered, then revise and edit the definition as the composing process unfolds.

Glossaries

Lesson on page 38.

A glossary is an alphabetical list of words with brief explanations, found in or relating to a specific subject or text. In some texts, a glossary is provided for words that are presented in a language other than English.

How-To

Lesson on page 41.

How-to writing involves giving directions or outlining procedures for readers to follow. How-to instructions are easy to follow when they are clear, accurate, complete, and exact, and when they list each step in order.

Teaching Tips

- Catherine Newman and illustrator Debbie Fong have written two graphic how-to books that offer readers advice on how to gain confidence and learn skills around getting along and responsibility: *How To Be A Person: 65 Hugely Useful, Super-Important Skills to Learn before You're Grown Up* and the sequel *What Can I Say? A Kid's Guide to Super-Useful Social Skills to Help You Get Along and Express Yourself.* Chapter titles include How to Have a Conversation, How to Get Along with People, and How to Care for Your Community.
- When giving instructions, outlining rules or explaining procedures, it is important for students to talk before writing. By turning to one or two partners to explain how to do something, students are given the opportunity to rehearse what they might put on paper. Talk can help students to consider sequence, completeness, and clarity of How-To writing.

Recipes

Lesson on page 64.

Recipes, whether found in cookbooks, in newspapers, magazines, or calendars or collected by families in boxes or binders, provide instructions on how to prepare food item or a favorite meal. Recipes need to list ingredients and the quantity needed for each item, suggest equipment needed, and provide step by step instructions on how to prepare an appetizer, a vegetable dish, a beverage, a dessert, a main course dish.

Teaching Tip

Many simple dishes can be prepared in the classroom or using the kitchen facilities in the school. Some snack dishes require no cooking (i.e., fruit salad, ice-cream sundae).

Rules

Lesson on page 67.

Rules are used to play a sport or game successfully. When beginning to play an unfamiliar game, it's important to know which rules to follow. Safety rules are written to ensure that order is kept in school, in the community, or during an event. Rules also need to be considered for living a life of responsibility and belonging.

Teaching Tips

- You can bring in written instructions for a board game, card game, or video game that students enjoy playing. Alternatively, you can use the internet to investigate written rules for unfamiliar games. In groups, students can examine the instructions to determine how easy they were to follow; what seems a bit puzzling; if the language of the rules are clear or some terms are unfamiliar; some good features of written rules.
- When you play games, rules need to be followed to enjoy the game. Rules are also needed to ensure that procedures are followed or that safety for all is considered. Have students discuss: Why do we have rules? What happens if rules are broken? How do they think rules should be decided upon? What are three rules they might consider for following rules?

Zodiac

Lesson on page 82.

The zodiac is made up of twelve signs named for the stellar constellations. By charting the signs of the zodiac, astrologists claim to be able to read character and foretell the future. Many people are intrigued to read daily horoscope predictions in newspapers or on the internet. When they write horoscopes, students are given an appealing and imaginative way to offer opinions.

Teaching Tips

- Use the Zodiac Charts reproducible on page 115 for this lesson.
- The Chinese zodiac plays an essential role in many Asian cultures. The 12 zodiac animals in a cycle are not only used to represent years in China, but also believed to influence people's personalities, career, compatibility, marriage, and fortune. Most students in any given class are born a year or two apart, so most students will likely have the same sign. You might suggest they investigate the Chinese zodiac sign for family members to add variety.

Writing to Inform/Inquire

Biographies

Lesson on page 19.

A biography is the life story of someone written by another person, and so is written in the third person. Biographies tell true stories about people by describing their lives, backgrounds, successes, achievements, and struggles. Writing biographies will give students the opportunity to research information and present facts, anecdotes, and visuals in an interesting way to inform others about that person's life.

Teaching Tip

There are a number of ways students can present biographical information. They may wish to present information

- using different headings, on separate pages

- including copies of photographs and/or creating illustrations to accompany their text
- outlining highlights of the person's life as a timeline
- as a digital story or digital slide show of the person's life

Essays

Lesson on page 31.

Essays provide writers with an opportunity to express their thoughts and feelings about a topic that interests them. Essays can also include research information to support an idea or ideas. Writing an essay helps students organize their thinking on a topic, and helps them understand the topic better and sort out feelings about it. When others read student essays, they come to know the topic better too.

Teaching Tips

- Because essay writing involves planning, developing, and revising over time, students can work in groups of two or three as an editorial group. Editors can serve as partners in the writing as they provide feedback, recommendations for additions or deletions, and suggestions for copy editing (i.e., spelling, grammar, punctuation).
- See also Essays to Persuade on page 92; lesson on page 32.

Interviews

Lesson on page 42.

Interviews are arranged meetings in which one or more persons question someone to get opinions or receive information. Interviews are a form of inquiry and research that requires effective listening, speaking, and questioning skills. It is an activity that connects talk and writing. Whether students record and then transcribe interviews, or take notes as they listen to the interviewee, writing interviews is a meaningful way for them to present information.

Teaching Tips

- Use the Question Matrix on page 109 for this lesson.
- Questioning is an essential skill. Remind students that, when they are conducting an interview, other questions might emerge that hadn't been prepared. When an interviewer is inspired to ask by something the interviewee has said, they can ask a probing question to get the speaker to elaborate.
- If students are conducting interviews with school staff, ensure that these people (custodian, librarian, secretary etc.) will be involved in only one interview.

KWL

Lesson on page 45.

KWL is a popular instructional strategy that helps students combine background knowledge with new information about a topic. It is ideally used to dig deep into content information about a science (e.g., animal habitats, electricity) or social studies topic (i.e., history or geography). Used in groups, KWL demonstrates to students that they are a community that can share information about a topic. It also creates a forum that builds curiosity and leads to further inquiry.

Teaching Tips

- The KWL chart can be an important minds-on activity when beginning exploration of some tough topics that will be explored over time: e.g., the

Residential School Experience, the Holocaust, mental health, global warming, prejudice, and discrimination.

- Ideally, the KWL strategy should span a thematic unit over time. The chart can be introduced before, during, and/or after reading. New questions and new information can be added to the chart through a variety of resources that students experience as the inquiry unfolds.

Newsletters

Lesson on page 55.

A newsletter is a tool used to share relevant and interesting information with an audience. In businesses, a newsletter can let customers and potential subscribers share content and promote sales for a company. In the classroom, a newsletter can be sent to families to summarize curriculum events, share student work, make announcements, and give shout-outs to classroom events and accomplishments of students in the class.

Teaching Tips

- The newsletter provides the opportunity to include various writing formats (e.g., lists, anecdotes, comic strips, interviews, etc.). Having their written work in a newsletter can be a motivator for students in revising and editing work, free of errors.
  Each student's name should appear at least once in every newsletter. A special feature can include can list student's names alphabetically and demonstrate how each student has participated; for example:

  We collected interesting words this month…
  Our favorite books this month are…

- Classroom newsletters should be sent out on a regular basis to families. Some teachers choose to send a weekly message, some might offer a monthly newsletter.

News Reports

Lesson on page 56.

A news report presents day to day events of interest that happen locally or globally. News reports (current events) are about people, places, and things and outline events and issues that are tragic or entertaining. Reports can cover a number of topics that include political, business, sports, entertainment, and community events. By writing a news report, students practice presenting information that answers the questions *Who? When? Where? What? Why?* and *How?*

Teaching Tips

- To write a news report, it is important that students read newspaper reports. Make available a copy of a daily newspaper (hard copy of digital), or bring in a fairly recent edition of a newspaper to share.
- The class can be organized to produce a newspaper published by the classroom. Students can sign on to be reporters by considering classroom events, school-wide events, local news, sports, entertainment, etc. The following outlines suggestions for organizing the class project:

  - The group votes on a name for their newspaper.
  - Reports can be written individually, in pairs, or as team.
  - A group of editors can be arranged to revise and edit written drafts.
  - Some members of the class can volunteer to be illustrators/photographers.

- Additional feature items can include interviews, announcements, advertisements, comics, puzzles, food/recipes.
- The internet provides templates for students to use to plan, develop, and publish a student newspaper.

Observations

Lesson on page 57.

Observations are a record of things we encounter in our everyday lives. When a writer knows a subject well, they can commit themselves to presenting thoughts to an audience. If material is exciting and clear to the writer, chances are it will be clear to a reader. Most people go through each day without paying attention to what is around them. Observations help writers to keep their minds, eyes, and ears open as they encounter the unique features of everyday realities. Observing and recording things in our environments can heighten a writer's sense of adding details and describing them effectively.

Teaching Tip

To promote the skill of making observations, provide one or more opportunities for students take a few moments to intentionally and carefully inspect and describe in detail an item that might otherwise be looked at casually. How would students describe the pen or pencil they are writing with, their knapsack, an apple, the shoes they are wearing today, a plant, the view from a window?

Questions

Lesson on page 59.

Questions are the stuff of curiosity, imagination, and inquiry. Questions or puzzlements can spur us to seek out answers and to add information to our bank of knowledge. Writing questions can stimulate students' minds and encourage them to use language effectively to ask questions that invite different levels of thinking. Writing questions helps to explore the comprehension strategy of questioning, in which students reflect on puzzlements and curiosities about a text. Writing questions also prepares them for inquiry, motivating students to seek answers about a topic of interest.

Quizzes

Lesson on page 61.

A quiz asks a series of questions used to test someone's knowledge about a topic. The answers to quizzes are usually short and can be used as a formative assessment or content review of a subject.

Teaching Tip

When working with others to develop quizzes, students participate in a talk task that promotes discussion, brainstorming, and negotiation.

Transcriptions

Lesson on page 74.

A transcription is a written record of oral talk, for example a conversation, an interview, a drama improvisation. Writing down speech gives students practice in listening carefully and paying attention to how language is used. When transcribing talk, they needn't focus on the composing process as much as they would with other writing forms, thus providing a chance to give attention to spelling, punctuation, and capitalization.

Teaching Tip

Transcribing conversations demands careful attention to the conventions of print. As students transcribe, they might not pay close attention to spelling, capitalization, and handwriting. Have students exchange writing with another pair who will then copyedit their paper, marking errors they find.

Xpert Writing

Lesson on page 80.

This lesson invites you to share information about a topic that you feel you know a lot about. Your expert knowledge might be drawn from a personal experience, a hobby, or a topic you know a lot about.

Teaching Tip

To extend the expert writing, encourage students to research their topic through print or digital texts. What additional information might they add to their expert piece? What are some descriptive details they might add to their writing?

Writing Narratives

Fables

Lesson on page 34.

Fables are short folktales that often use animals to represent certain human types and end in a simple moral or lesson. A fable, like other narratives, has a plot, characters, a problem, and a solution.

Teaching Tip

Encourage students to revise their fables by considering the following:

- How do the animal characters behave/speak like animals?
- How effectively have characters and setting been described?
- How has dialogue been used effectively within the story?
- Does the story have a sequence of events with a clear beginning and end?
- What moral or lesson does the fable teach? Is it clearly stated at the end?

Mysteries

Lesson on page 52.

Mystery is a fiction genre where the nature of an event, usually a murder or other crime, remains mysterious until the end of the story. In fiction, characters find themselves solving some kind of problem. In mystery stories, the problem to be solved is the mystery. There are many types of mystery stories: stories about crimes, missing characters, sudden appearance of strange objects or characters, or people being pursued. Writing mysteries provides students with the opportunity to sharpen their narrative skills by inventing interesting characters, vividly describing a setting, and introducing a problem. Sequencing, suspense, and vivid description help keep a reader guessing and reading on until the mystery is solved (or not).

Teaching Tip

Authors often intentionally create a feeling of tension and curiosity in their readers. Tell students that one way of creating suspense is to give the reader clues about what will happen in the story, but to not give everything away. This makes the reader interested in finding out what will happen next. Also, providing an explanation of foreshadowing—a literary device in which a writer gives an advance hint of what is to come later in the story—can help students understand how to create suspense that encourages readers to continue reading to discover how events unfold.

Myths

Lesson on page 53.

Myths are invented stories, created hundreds or thousands of years ago that helped people to accept natural events that seemed mysterious or strange to them. Myths try to explain natural phenomena that affect people, and problems involved in relationships, usually through the actions or intervention of gods or other supernatural beings. Myths have grown slowly from the needs of particular nations or peoples. Most myths took many, many years to develop. By imitating and experimenting with myth narratives, students will have opportunities to make up stories of their own.

Teaching Tip

As the stories are told and retold they became exaggerated. A legend is likely to be less concerned with deities and the supernatural than myth, but legend and myth are related as narratives concerning a real person, event, or place. Some defining feature of legends:

- Generally told to explain a belief or something in nature
- Often glorify someone who performed great deeds or caused marvelous things to happen
- Describe an adventure
- Sometimes include magic
- Sometimes depict the struggle between good and evil

Urban Tales

Lesson on page 75.

Urban tales are unbelievable, humorous, adventurous stories that could be true. They are presented as stories that have been passed down over the years. The more the story is retold, the more it might change. Stories about ghosts that are passed on from generation to generation can often be considered the stuff of an urban tale.

Teaching Tip

Students may have stories told within their families about strange things that have happened in their homes or communities. After retelling these stories to classmates, in groups, or the whole class, they can then preserve the story by writing it as an urban tale.

Yarns

Lesson on page 81.

A yarn is a kind of humorous tale of made-up events. Yarns are told in everyday speech and they usually about wild impossible adventures.

Teaching Tips

- Use the Tic-Tac-Toe Chart reproducible on page 114 for this lesson.
- Students might have told or heard stories that are not true but are made to sound like they are. Many of these yarn stories are told orally, but when written for others to read they can be entertaining and intriguing, as they keep the reader guessing if they are really true.

Writing Opinions

Advertisements

Lesson on page15.

The goal of advertising is to persuade people to buy a certain product or to sell an idea. A successful ad—in a newspaper, magazine, billboard, or website—attracts attention with clever design or presentation, often using effective words or slogans to get across the message.

Commercials

Lesson on page 26.

A commercial is a video advertisement aired on TV, on the radio, at a movie, or online to sell a product or inform an audience about a business or a service.

Teaching Tip

Students will be familiar with short videos, but commercials have an informational and persuasive component that might be missing from social media clips. Invite students to think how video elements, such as music and action, can make commercials more effective.

Essays to Persuade

Lesson on page 32.

Essays provide writers with an opportunity to express their thoughts and feelings about a topic that interests them. An essay is personal; it invites writers to share their knowledge and insights about a topic. Writing an essay helps students organize their thinking, better understand the topic, and sort out feelings about it.

Teaching Tips

- Some suggestions for essay topics students might feel strongly about:

    - Global Warming is Everyone's Responsibility
    - Everyone Has A Right to an Education
    - Diversity Matters
    - My Country is a Wonderful Country to Live In
    - When Bystanders become Upstanders
    - Video Games Can Make You Smarter: Can't They?
    - Mindfulness
    - Everything I Know About Life I Learned from…

- See also Essays on page 87, lesson on page 31.

Excuses

Lesson on page 33.

Excuses are made up reasons that we often use to get out of doing something, or not having done something that we were expected to do. Sometimes we make excuses even though the other person knows they are not really true.

Teaching Tip

Students can present their written excuses as real-life, believable reasons, or perhaps create excuses that may be considered unbelievable or demonstrate "outside the box" thinking.

Letters to Persuade

Lesson on page 48.

Persuasive letter-writing encourages students to state a position and justify it. Being able to express an opinion clearly and give supportive reasons to back it up is an essential real-world writing skill for students to practice and develop. Persuasive writing at a glance:

With thanks to Adrienne Gear.

- To give a point of view
- To justify a position
- To persuade or convince your reader of an idea you want them to agree to
- To encourage readers to purchase something, participate in a specific activity, or think in a certain way
- Provides four to six strong reasons to support a writer's views

Teaching Tips

- Mentor books serve as important models for persuasive writing. *I Wanna Iguana* by Karen Kaufman Orloff can be read to inspire students to write letters to parents to convince them that they need a new pet. Orloff's story effectively provides evidence of supportive arguments that can serve as a model for student writing.
- Like advertisements, persuasive letters can be written to sell a product or an idea. Students can write a persuasive letters to

  - convince others to buy a product
  - promote a book they have enjoyed reading
  - sell an idea to a teacher or school administrator (e.g., more time for recess; wearing school uniforms; having only healthy snacks in the school; a fund-raising initiative etc.)

- See also Letters on page 99, lesson on page 46; Letters in Role on page 105, lesson on page 47.

Reviews

Lesson on page 66.

A review can help us decide whether we are interested in reading a book, seeing a movie or show, or listening to music. A review often provides a synopsis of the work and highlights features of it (e.g., format, style, visuals, information about the creator). Whether a review is presented in newspapers, online, or from someone we know, a reviewer's opinions can motivate readers to pick up the book, watch, or listen to enjoy—or not.

Teaching Tips

- Introduce students to websites like Amazon and Goodreads that invite readers to share their opinions of books.
- You can extend students' book review experience by inviting them to write a review of examples of media other than books: e.g., TV shows, movies, plays, concerts, recitals, YouTube videos.

Surveys

Lesson on page 70.

Surveys are prepared to get people's opinions about a topic or issue. Often information gathered by interviewing a number of people can be presented as a survey. Interviews conducted on paper are called questionnaires. Surveys are an important tool to use when exploring the math strand of Data Management and Probability.

Teaching Tip

The results of a survey or questionnaire can be presented as a graph to summarize information that was learned by asking questions of a number of people. Once completed, have students present the results of a focus question as a bar graph.

Writing Patterns

Alphabet Books

Lesson on page 16.

Alphabet Books follow a pattern, are usually based on theme or topic, and give information with words and pictures to engage readers of all ages. Some alphabet books might have one word on a page, others might have a syntactic pattern that is continued throughout the book. By creating an alphabet book, students will have the chance to create an illustrated picture book to share, perhaps with children in a younger grade.

Teaching Tip

- Some patterns students might notice in alphabet books:

  - One word per page: e.g., *Apples, Bananas, Cucumbers, Dates*, etc.
  - Simple sentence: e.g., *A is for Aardvark.*
  - Alliteration: e.g., *The lion lounges lazily near the little lake.*
  - Names of people and/or places: e.g., *Alex lives in Alberta.*
  - Feature word + information: e.g., *A is for Activist. An activist a person who campaigns to bring about social or political change.*

Dialogue

Lesson on page 28.

Dialogue is a conversation between two or more people as a feature of a book, play, or movie. There are three essential ways to write dialogue:

- Conversation
  "Are you still there?"
  "Are you?"
  "Why didn't you hang up?"
  "Why didn't you?"
- Script
  Joshua: Are you still there?
  Ayla: Are you?
  Joshua: Why didn't you hang up?
  Ayla: Why didn't you?
- Speech bubbles

Teaching Tip

Depending on the needs of students, you can choose to teach rules about writing dialogue in their stories. For example:

- Adding explanation words (*said, replied, asked, announced*, etc.):
- Breaking a line of dialogue: e.g., *"I think you should hurry,"* Mother announced, *"because your bus is here."*

Graphic Texts

Lesson on page 39.

Graphic texts are easily recognizable by their storyboard or comic-book presentation. A story is told through illustrations, dialogue and thought balloons, and narrative captions. There are multi-genre approaches to graphic texts, including adventure, fantasy, realistic fiction, science fiction, and autobiography. When students create comic strips or graphic stories and manga (the Japanese word for comic book), they have the opportunity to compose texts using illustration and verbal text; to consider sequencing; to present dialogue; and to use technology to support and extend their writing skills.

Teaching Tip

Pixton EDU is an application for teachers and students that allows users to create comics and storyboards. This popular tool is way for students to create media to respond to something they have read, a curriculum topic they have investigated, or a narrative story they have created. Pixton users can use their imaginations to manipulate characters and to form images, add verbal text, and record voices.

Jokes

Lesson on page 43.

Jokes, oral and written, are anecdotes that people tell to cause amusement or laughter, especially a story with a funny punchline. Joke-telling is an ideal strategy for having students transcribe oral conversation into print. Since they are not concerned with the composing stage, writing jokes and riddles allows them to demonstrate their knowledge of writing sentences, writing dialogue, using punctuation, and writing short narrative paragraphs.

Teaching Tips

- Review the rules of writing dialogue (see page 00). Knock-knock jokes and question-and-answer riddles are two forms of dialogue that let students practice writing conversation and using question marks, periods, and exclamation points.
- Students can write four or five jokes or riddles and then survey others to investigate which they think is the funniest of the selection. The data could be graphed.

Lists

Lesson on page 49.

A list is a series of words selected by a writer for a particular purpose. A list can be arranged consecutively, chronologically, or randomly. Writing lists can tap into students' prior knowledge and experiences, as well as provide a reason to use their spelling and vocabulary skills.

Teaching Tips

- The List Race activity could be repeated with a new list topic to brainstorm and a longer time limit for the list race.
- Other listing activities:

  - The Books of My Life: Each student creates a list of ten titles that they have enjoyed reading, then identify three favorite titles, and then put an asterisk beside the one title that can be considered an all-time favorite.
  - A Few of My Favorite Things: Students prepare a list of five favorite items for three of these categories: favorite candies, favorite TV shows, favorite

singers or musical groups, favorite animals, favorite authors, favorite song titles, favorite games, favorite movies.

- Things I Know About: Working independently or with one or two classmates, students choose one of the following topics and make a list of things they know about this topic; hair, makeup, hockey (or any sport), baking, playing a musical instrument, spreading kindness, whales (or any animal).

Patterns

Lesson on page 58.

Pattern stories follow a sequential pattern that is repeated throughout the book. Pattern picture books can become mentor texts for students to hitchhike their writing on. Writing an innovation on the pattern is a way to build sight vocabulary and fluency, as well as to explore how verbal and visual text are formatted to bring meaning to a page.

Teaching Tips

- Explicit instruction is needed to ensure that students understand and follow the author's original pattern. This is best done by displaying a fill-in-the-blank pattern and soliciting suggestions of words and phrases that might be included to create a new, original text.
- Creating collaborative pattern books is a useful bookmaking activity that builds community, puts the writing process into action, and offers a book to be read by class members (and others in the school community) as a shared reading or independent reading experience. Collaborative books can be transformed into digital format, with each student's page featured as a slide in a slide presentation.

Scripts for Readers Theatre

Lesson on page 68.

A script tells a story through the speech of characters in a play. The actors use the script to help the audience understand the action, meaning, and mood of the play. In Readers Theatre, a script is developed from material not initially written for performance. This is a meaningful way to introduce both script writing and interpretation. Readers Theatre does not require participants to memorize a selection. Before reading the text aloud, group members should think about and discuss the way narration and dialogue can be divided among group members.

Teaching Tips

- You can present students with an example of original text and the Readers Theatre script, like this excerpt from the novel *Ground Zero* by Alan Gratz. In this novel, a young boy named Brandon is trapped in the collapse of the World Trade Center on September 11, 2001.

A white Port Authority policewoman with her hair in a brown ponytail pointed them toward the staircase.

"Wait, doesn't this go to the basement?" Richard asked. "Why can't we just go outside?"

"We can't take you through the lobby. It's too full of injured people. And it's dangerous right outside the building."

Brandon knew why. Outside through the window he could still hear what sounded like pebbles and stones raining down on the concrete plaza.

Narrator: A white Port Authority policewoman with her hair in a brown ponytail pointed them toward the staircase.
Richard: Wait, doesn't this go to the basement?" Why can't we just go outside?
Policewoman: We can't take you through the lobby. It's too full of injured people. And it's dangerous right outside the building.
Narrator: Brandon knew why. Outside through the window he could still hear what sounded like pebbles and stones raining down on the concrete plaza.

- An alternative way for students to write scripts using dialogue from a novel is to have them present the excerpt as a theatre script, without narration.

Richard: Wait, doesn't this go to the basement? Why can't we just go outside?
Policewoman: We can't take you through the lobby. It's too full of injured people.

- An essential extension of writing scripts is to have students read their writing out loud. Give students the opportunity rehearse the script by assigning different students to read the roles of different characters.

Titles

Lesson on page 73.

"You gotta put something out there that gets their attention and gets them curious."—James Patterson

Titles are an important text feature that help readers to make a prediction about books they are going to read or movies they might want to see. By investigating and writing titles, students can consider the careful choice of words used to summarize the narrative or content. In this way, they can consider the use of titles in their own written work.

Teaching Tips

- The Read to Write activity can be repeated by students working in small groups of four or five. Each member can bring two or three novel titles for the group to discuss.
- Emphasize to students that correct punctuation is an important part of writing titles. The first word is always written in upper case. Most words written in a title should begin with an upper case letter, especially names of people, places, and things.

Word Games/Word Power

Lessons on pages 77 and 78.

"Reach for your own words to tell the world who you are and how you will make it better."—Peter H. Reynolds, *The Word Collector*

Writing cannot happen without words. It is a creative process that involves arranging and rearranging words. The more words students know, the wider the net for them to choose from in their writing, and the deeper the understanding can be of the power of the word. The activities in these lessons offer suggestions to enrich students' understanding of spelling patterns and vocabulary choices.

Teaching Tips

- These activities can be worked on independently, in pairs, or in small groups.
- Some games can be played as a competition. Organize students into groups and challenge them to complete the word lists within a time limit. Keeping score to determine which group has the most words is optional.

Personal Writing

Autobiographies

Lesson on page 18.

An autobiography results when someone writes about their own life. An autobiography can tell things that have happened in the past. An autobiography is a chance for students to look into the rear-view mirror of their life, giving important information and highlighting significant events by telling stories about those events. The word *autobiography* comes from the Greek: *autos* (meaning "self") and *bios* (meaning "life").

Teaching Tip

There is a sequel to *Fatty Legs* entitled *A Stranger at Home,* as well as two picture book versions of Margaret-Olemaun Pokiak-Fenton's story: *When I Was Eight* and *Not My Girl,* both illustrated by Gabrielle Grimard.

Diaries

Lesson on page 29.

A diary is a day-by-day record someone writes about their life. A diary can recount what has happened to the writer on a particular day, what they saw and heard, and often their thoughts and feelings about daily events.

Teaching Tips

- Since diary writing is personal, invite students to voluntarily share particular entries with friends or with you.
- Invite students to become characters in a story they've read or step into the shoes of an important person from history or science or the arts. Have them imagine that this person kept a diary and prepare an entry or series of entries from this character or person's point of view.

Journals

Lesson on page 44.

Journals demonstrate a writer's ownership and place students at the centre of their learning. Journal entries help them to reflect and make connections between new and prior knowledge; serve as a connection between reading and writing; and can serve as a connector between home and school. Journals can come in all shapes and sizes. Choosing what to write in a journal is essential to the practice of journal-writing.

- Use the Thought Starters list on page 117 to provide students with prompts for writing.

Teaching Tips

- Journal writing is not a one-time lesson. Consider the following to establish a meaningful writing program with journals:

  - Implementing journals into the program requires consistency.
  - A designated time should be integrated into the timetable to have students write in their journals.
  - Students can choose to record thoughts in a variety of curriculum areas.
  - They can write in their journals outside the classroom.
  - A specific prompt or question can be introduced for the class to respond to.
  - When a routine of journal-writing is established, you should ensure that students have choice in what they want to write on a particular day. Some entries can be carried over several days.

- Journal entries can be consider draft writing. They can choose to revise and edit their work for spelling, grammar, and punctuation.

Letters

Lesson on page 46.

Letters are written for many reasons: to let others know what's happening, to thank someone for a gift, to recount travel experiences, etc. In modern times, the art of personal letter-writing is gradually fading. By writing personal letters, students can practice the text features particular to this writing form. This will give them practice in writing letters for professional and business purposes (e.g., job applications, letters of complaint, persuasive letters, etc.)

Teaching Tips

- As students explore letter-writing, ensure that they have the opportunity to actually send the letter to the person they write to. An envelope and stamp might be necessary to post some letters. Alternatively, some letters can be delivered in person (e.g., to the teacher, a community member, a friend, a family member).
- See also Letters to Persuade on page 92, lesson on page 48; Letters in Role on page 104, lesson on page 47.

Memoirs

Lesson on page 51.

A memoir is a written memory of an incident in our lives. Memories are very close to us and what we are. It is, therefore, significant that students tell stories and preserve stories in order to help them reflect on their memories and their significance.

"When we celebrate the stories of children's lives, we blur the lines between home and school and let the students know that their lives matter."—Regie Routman (2018)

"Storytelling is a means of reflecting, comprehending and validating the self."—Jason Reynolds

Teaching Tips

- Use the From Word to Story: An ABC list on page 107 for this lesson.
- Use the Thought Starters list on page 117 to provide students with prompts for writing.
- A strong strategy to consider is students putting thoughts down on paper, or oral narratives. In the classroom, students can tell stories to a partner, in small groups, to the whole class community, or perhaps privately to the teacher. To encourage oral narrative:

Before the story: Activate prior experience by saying "This is a story about… Does anyone have a story to share about this topic?"
During the story: Encourage spontaneous response; we cannot predict or plan for what will trigger a memory.
After the story: Ask, "Was there anything in the story (a word, a picture, an artifact) that reminded you of something from your own life, or someone you know?'

- Since memoir writing is in the first person, it can be a significant strategy for having students develop voice in their writing (see also page 101). The stories that students share orally in preparation for writing memoirs provide strong impetus for developing voice in their memoir writing.
- When making connections to a topic or story, students might think of similar incidents from their own lives. Making connections to stories of someone they know is also part of their personal narrative.

Name Stories

Lesson on page 54.

Names are "artifacts of our identities." (Belarie Zatzman).

Everyone has a name. Behind every name is a story. When we ask about their names, we are inviting students to think about the how they got their names, the significance of the name, the meaning behind their names, and sometimes the challenges of spelling or pronouncing their names. Recalling personal narratives about their names, sharing them orally with others, and then writing these stories help students connect to their identities and cultures, and connect to each other.

Teaching Tips

- Use the What's Your Name reproducible on page 108 for this lesson.
- Some sample names stories you could share with students:

My name is Mia and I love it! My parents were going to name me Summer because I was born on summer solstice. I'm glad they named me Mia.

My mom and dad named me Jeremy. They told me that when I was born, they each decided to make a list of three names they liked. They both had the name Jeremy on it.

My name is Georgia. In Latin it means 'farmer's daughter'. My parents chose the name because my dad LOVES music (me too!). When my mom was thinking of a name for a girl, she thought of Georgia and of course my dad loved it because of the jazzy song "Georgia on my mind."

Once upon a time there was a kid blessed by God, and thus was born Adam.

Quickwrites

Lesson on page 60.

Quickwriting is an exercise that encourages spontaneous writing in response to a question or topic of interest. It is an impromptu experience where students are given a short period of time (five to ten minutes) to let their thoughts flow freely on the page, without pausing to address spelling or to make revisions.

Teaching Tips

- Quickwrites can be introduced a number of times within a month. Offer a question, statement, or topic and give students time to experience a quickwrite. Students can then choose a quickwrite piece they would like to spend more time with and move to publication.
- You can use the From Word to Story: An ABC list on page 107 to prompt student quickwrites.

Recounts

Lesson on page 65.

A recount is the retelling or recounting of an event or a experience. The purpose is to tell what happened, often based on the direct experience of the writer. Recounts, though often personal, can also be factual or imaginative.

Teaching Tips

- Use the Recount Checklist on page 112 for this lesson.
- To prepare to write recounts of events that have personally happened to them, have students work with one or two classmates to tell their story before writing. This oral recount is a worthwhile rehearsal for putting thought on paper. Oral recounts help students think about what happened,

the order of events, and the descriptive details that can help make the story come alive.

- An important component of recounts is presenting ideas in chronological order. Provide an anchor chart of sequential words that students might consider using:

Beginning
Once / To begin / First of all / It all started
Middle
Then/ Next / Soon / Eventually / Suddenly / Meanwhile / Later
End
At last / Finally / Lastly

Social Media

Lesson on page 69.

Social media are computer-based technologies that facilitate the sharing of ideas, thoughts, and information. By design, social media are Internet-based and give users quick electronic communication of content through virtual networks; e.g., blogs, email, texting, social networks (Twitter, Instagram, TikTok, etc.).

Teaching Tip

Responsible use of social media is critical for everyone today. It is important to review and reinforce the rules and responsible use of social media. Since cyberbullying mostly happens mostly outside the class, have a class discussion on how to handle situations where someone writes something inappropriate online.

Thank-You Messages

Lesson on page 71.

Thank-you messages are a form of personal writing that is a demonstration of gratitude. Notes could be written to thank someone for a gift, as an appreciation of receiving a donation, or as an appreciation of a favor or kindness. Thank-you notes serve as an authentic piece of writing to be read by an audience.

Teaching Tip

In most cases, students will know the person they are sending the note to. In some cases, thank-you notes could be sent to strangers who have put forth a special effort for the community. During the pandemic, some students wrote thank-you notes to front line workers to thank them for their service. During the clean-up of the building disaster in Florida in 2021, children wrote notes to anonymous workers who worked tirelessly in an attempt to rescue survivors. Who, in the school, or local community, might students send thank-you notes to for deeds small or large?

Voice

Lesson on page 76.

Voice is at the heart of writing. When we read good writing we "hear" the sound of another human talking to us. Author Ralph Fletcher defines voice in writing as "personality on paper." Unique use of language, the sharing of feelings, and including reactions are ways to add spark and voice to writing.

Teaching Tip

Writing in the first person often introduces a personal relationship between the writer and the material. When stories are told in the first person, readers often get inside the character's head.

Writing Poems

Blackout Poems

Lesson on page 20.

Blackout poetry is when a page of text—a newspaper article, for example—is completely blacked out (i.e., colored over with permanent marker so that it is no longer visible) except for a select few words. When only these words are visible, a free verse poem can be created from the existing text. Blackout poetry is a type of found poetry that is also known as reductive poetry or erasure poetry.

Teaching Tip

- Encourage students to choose a minimum number of words; e.g., a maximum of 20. Once they have gone through the blackout process, they can review the text at least one more time, continuing to eliminate words.
- There are several demonstrations of the blackout process to be found on YouTube.

Cinquain Poems

Lesson on page 25.

A cinquain (*SANG-kane*) is an unrhymed shape poem composed of five lines (the word for "five" in French is *cinq*). Each line of the poem has a special purpose. By following rules and guidelines for each line, students can have fun playing with words and arranging them into cinquains.

Teaching Tip

To extend the work with cinquains, students can move beyond writing about people by considering one of the following topics for cinquain poems:

- a favorite food
- a favorite sport
- a possession
- a pet
- an animal
- nature (e.g., a tree, a cloud, a river)

Formula Poems

Lesson on page 35.

Formula poems invite writers to play with patterns, manipulate words, count syllables, or comply with a specific metre or rhythm. Writing in this way becomes a puzzle for students to solve as they mold words and release their imagination.

Teaching Tips

- Cinquain (p. 102), haiku (p. 103), and list poems (p. 103) are three types of formula poems that are written according to rules.
- Give students opportunities, over time, to create different formula poems. They can then choose a favorite poem they have written and present a final copy, perhaps illustrated. A class poetry anthology can be created, with each student contributing at least one poem to the collection.

Free Verse Poems

Lesson on page 37.

Traditional poetry usually has a set form. It is organized in set stanzas having regular rhythm patterns and often regular rhyme schemes. Free verse doesn't have these restrictions. The lines have no set length in terms of a fixed number of syllables. Free verse lacks the predictable rhythms established by a predetermined pattern. Rhyming is optional. Free verse poetry allows the poet to express feelings and ideas without being restricted by the rules of traditional metrical forms. In free verse, the writer develops their own rules of form for each new poem written.

Gaining popularity over the past two decades has been the free verse novel, usually a series of free verse poems presented in a sequence that builds a narrative. Each poem is usually no more than two or three pages in length. By investigating free verse novels, students will have rich opportunities to experience this poetry form, to understand and appreciate the form, and to perhaps be motivated to write their own free verse.

Teaching Tips

- To help students investigate the choices a poet makes in arranging words on a page, supply students with a non-rhyming poem you have reformatted as prose. Students work in pairs to rearrange the lines the way that they think they were originally written in free verse format.
- Recommended free verse novels:

Brown Girl Dreaming by Jacqueline Woodson
The Crazy Man by Pamela Porter
Ebb and Flow by Heather Smith
Home of the Brave by Katherine Applegate
Inside Out and Back Again by Thanhha Lai

Haiku

Lesson on page 40.

Haiku are three-line poems composed of carefully chosen words to present a picture that is full of mood and feeling. These poems, first written in Japan, describe the world around us and often express how we feel about nature and the environment. Haiku most often follow a pattern of 17 syllables.

Teaching Tip

To write haiku, it is important for students to read and respond to the qualities of these short poems. Have students use the internet or find poetry books that present examples of a few haiku poems and have them consider: Which haiku is your favorite? Do they each follow the 5–7–5 rule? Which words created the strongest impact?

List Poems

Lesson on page 50.

A list is a series of words selected by a writer for a particular purpose. By placing the words on a page in an interesting way, writers can create patterns that have the power of a poem. Often, following a syntactic pattern can make an ordinary list into poetry.

Teaching Tip

Poems can be illustrated (or accompanied with a photograph) and displayed on a class website or bulletin board, or in a class blog. A digital presentation of portrait poems can be created with each student contributing one "I am…" statement that best represents them.

Writing to Respond to Reading

Book Blurbs

Lesson on page 21.

A book blurb appears on the back cover of the majority of paperback fiction, or on the book jacket of a hardback book. A blurb is intended to intrigue readers by giving them just enough information to persuade them to read the book. Writing a book blurb is an activity that encourages students to summarize a text they have read.

Teaching Tip

Two or more students can write a blurb for the same book. Once completed, they can compare their work. They might then collaborate to create a new piece by synthesizing ideas.

Character Journals

Lesson on page 24.

Character journals invite readers to imagine that they are a character from a book they have read who keeps a diary or journal to record their thoughts or feelings about events, relationships, and problems. Writing a journal entry from a character's perspective enables each reader to have a conversation with the text, giving the reader as much responsibility as the author in the making of meaning. Character journals are significant in building the reading-writing connection.

Teaching Tip

An important follow-up to character journal written assignments is for students to share responses with others by working in role. In this way, the activity promotes talk response to the reading and writing experience, while it initiates drama exploration through improvised, in-role conversations. Working in pairs, students can take turns interviewing a novel character.

Epilogues

Lesson on page 30.

An epilogue is a literary device that functions as a supplemental, but separate, part of the main story. An epilogue, usually a few pages in length, is mostly used to reveal the fates of the characters in a story and wrap up any loose ends.

Teaching Tip

Many writers think that if their book has a prologue, it must be balanced with an epilogue, or vice versa. But that isn't the case at all! A book can have only a prologue or only an epilogue.

Four-Rectangle Response

Lesson on page 36.

Four Rectangles is a graphic organizer used to write a response after reading or listening to a story, a poem, an article, or media like audio or video. The Four-Rectangle activity invites students to reflect on a text and personally respond to it in writing. Because the rectangle space is somewhat limited, students will likely not be intimidated by the thought of having to write a lot. By sharing your responses in small groups, students can discover whether others' opinions and/or connections were similar to or different from their own. The strategy provides a context for them to put thoughts on paper before sharing opinions with others through talk.

Teaching Tip

This activity works best if students are organized into groups of three. Students begin by writing a response in first rectangle. The response is then passed to another person who writes a response in a second rectangle. A third person reads responses written by #1 and #2 and then writes their response in a third rectangle. The paper is returned to the original writer who reads all three responses and writes a final response in the fourth rectangle. Allowing three to four minutes for each written response encourages students to fill in the space with more than one thought.

Letters in Role

Lesson on page 47

Writing letters in role invites writers to pretend to be someone else and send correspondence to another person. By stepping into the shoes of a fictional character, students can send a message from that person's point of view and recount events or present a problem.

Teaching Tip

See also Letters on page 99, lesson on page 46; Letters to Persuade on page 93, lesson on page 48.

Quotations

Lesson on page 62

Quotations are inspirational words that offer an authoritative voice to support an idea or issue. After reading quotations, students can share their personal connections to the sayings of others and reflect on the message offered by an authority, whether it's an author, a celebrity, a philosopher, an educator, etc.

Teaching Tip

Use the Writers on Writing list of quotations on page 110 for this lesson.

Reading Response Journals

Lesson on page 63.

The reading response journal is a vehicle for students to communicate thoughts and feelings about texts they are reading. Response entries can be about any text they have read, but when used as a record of novels, students are given opportunities to contemplate and reflect on a book over time. Journals are a medium for them to record their "in the head" responses as they read, as well as to consider effective reactions to the impact of the selection. The personal voice and choice of journal entries provide evidence of students' insights, questions, and reactions to books.

Teaching Tips

- Use the Journal Prompts reproducible on page 111 for this lesson.
- There are several ways in which you can facilitate exchange of journals:

  - You can invite students to share their journals with you.
  - You can establish a system where assigned reading buddies exchange entries.
  - You can ask students to place sticky notes on journal excerpts, inviting focused response for specific items.
  - Have students meet in groups of four or five to share entries of their choice. As group members discuss responses, they can ask questions, make connections, or offer opinions of what has been read.

- You may prompt students to share journal entries with a parent or other adult.

Thinking Stems

Lesson on page 72.

Thinking stems, or prompts, invite students to respond to in writing. They are a useful way to have students reflect on their reading and reveal their responses on paper. Using prompts is a convenient strategy for honoring individual personal response to a text where answers can be open-ended.

Teaching Tips

- Use the Thinking Stems Sample Prompts list on page 113 for this lesson.
- Thinking stems serve to break students free of the idea that there is one correct answer. When students collaborate with others to share and compare responses, they can discover viewpoints that may be different from their own. Thinking stems have students talk about their writing—and their reading!

Writing in Role

Lesson on page 79.

Writing in role is writing from a character's perspective in a familiar format such as a letter, email, diary, or text. Students are invited to step into another's shoes and examine the world from that point of view. Writing from a different perspective can deepen understanding of the character and help to develop empathy for the character and the situation.

Teaching Tips

- The picture book *The True Story of the Three Little Pigs* by Jon Scieszka, illustrated by Lane Smith, is an ideal example of writing in role. The author has taken a familiar story and re-told story events from a single character's point of view.
- Using Technology in Role: Have students work with a partner or a small group and exchange in-role text messages or e-mails. These messages might retell events, reveal problems, raise questions. The activity can be done with students becoming characters from a novel, or from two different novels. Allow about 10 minutes to create a text message exchange. Then, as a follow-up, students can read aloud the text messages as dialogue script, with each partner taking on a role. The text message dialogue can be transformed into a script to be rehearsed and presented.

From Word to Story: An ABC List

Every word can lead to a story. Any word from this alphabetical list can inspire you to quickwrite from your past to the memoir of your life,

Nouns	Verbs	Adjectives
adventure	anger	awesome
bully	bore	brave
camp	confuse	curious
disaster	dread	daring
eating	embarrass	elegant
fire	fear	fun
garden	gossip	grumpy
hospital	hope	helpful
illness	insult	interesting
joy	joke	jealous
keepsake	know	kind
laughter	love	lazy
movies	move	magnificent
neighbors	neglect	naughty
office	open	original
phobia	pity	powerful
quiet	question	quirky
religion	rest	responsible
scar	surprise	strange
tear	trust	triumphant
underneath	understand	unique
vacation	value	vain
writing	worry	wild
xylophone	x-ray	"xpert"
yesterday	yearn	young
zoo	zigzag	zany

Pembroke Publishers ©2022 *Write to Read* by Larry Swartz ISBN 978-1-55138-359-0

What's Your Name?

1. What is your full name?

2. Why did your parents choose to give you this name?

3. Were you named after someone? Who?

4. Do you have nickname? How did you get it?

5. Do you like your name? Why?

6. Do you know your name in other languages?

7. If you could choose another name, what might it be? Why?

8. What, if anything, is unique about the spelling of your first name? Of your last name?

9. Do you know the meaning of your name? If so, what does it mean?

10. List any family members, celebrities, historical figures, authors, or fictional characters who share your first name with you.

Bonus: How many words can you make using the letters from your first and last names?

Pembroke Publishers ©2022 *Write to Read* by Larry Swartz ISBN 978-1-55138-359-0

Question Matrix

	Who	What	Where	When	Why	How
is						
did						
can						
might						
would						
will						

Pembroke Publishers ©2022 *Write to Read* by Larry Swartz ISBN 978-1-55138-359-0

Writers on Writing

Let us remember: One book, one pen, one child and one teacher can change the world.
—Malala Yousafzai, activist, author

Read something, then write something. Read something else, then write something else.
—Marvin Bell, poet

There is something about writing the first words of a story because you never know where they will take you.
—Beatrix Potter

It all began when a teacher said, "Why don't you write that story down?"
—Kathy Kacer

You can make anything by writing.
—C.S. Lewis

I write to discover what I know.
—Flannery O'Connor

If you don't have time to read, you don't have the time (or the tools) to write. Simple as that.
—Stephen King

I can shake off everything as I write; my sorrows disappear, my courage is reborn.
—Anne Frank

There's always room for a story that can transport people to another place.
—J.K. Rowling

The most important thing anybody ever told me about writing was to write what you know and the only way to get to know things is to do your homework and research before you write.
—Eric Walters

Writing is like any sort of sport. In order for you to get better at it, you have to exercise the muscle.
—Jason Reynolds

It's not about what it is, it's about what it can become.
—Dr. Seuss

I think if everyone would write down the funny stories from their own childhoods, the world would be a better place.
—Jeff Kinney

I think the more you write, the more confident you get.
—Katherine Applegate

So the writer who breeds more words than he needs is making a chore for the reader who reads.
—Dr. Seuss

A writer has the duty to be good, not lousy; true, not false; lively, not dull; accurate, not full of error. He should tend to lift people up, not lower them down. Writers do not merely reflect and interpret life, they inform and shape life.
—E.B. White

You don't write because you want to, but because you have to.
—Judy Blume

Good writing is essentially rewriting. I'm positive of this.
—Roald Dahl

Pembroke Publishers ©2022 *Write to Read* by Larry Swartz ISBN 978-1-55138-359-0

Journal Prompts

1. What did you enjoy (or not enjoy) about what you read?

2. What, if anything, puzzled you as you read? What questions came to mind?

3. As you read, what did you see in your mind? (optional: create an illustration).

4. What problems unfolded in the novel? How do you think these problems will be resolved?

5. What words, phrases, sentences, or images made an impression on you? How did they do that?

6. What interests you (or doesn't interest you) about the characters in the novel?

7. How do the events and issues in the novel connect to your own experiences or those of someone you know?

8. What information did you learn from reading the novel? What might you want to know more about?

9. How do you feel about the way the author presented the story?

10. What do you predict might happen to the future lives of the characters?

11. What did you wonder about as you read the novel? Finished the novel?

12. What did you learn about yourself as a reader?

13. If this novel were made into a movie, describe a scene(s) that you would look forward to seeing.

14. On a scale of 1 to 10, how would you rate this book? Explain.

15. What might you tell others about what you have read?

Recount Checklist

Part A: Consider some of the questions your audience might ask while reading your recount:

☐ What occurred?

☐ Where did it take place?

☐ When did it occur?

☐ Who were the main characters/people involved?

☐ Why did certain things happen?

☐ How did things happen?

☐ What were some of your reactions to the events that occurred?

☐ What are the concluding thoughts or ideas you are left with as a reader?

PART B: Answer Strongly Agree (SA), Agree (A), Disagree (D)

I included all important information about what happened to me.	SA	A	D
My recount has a good beginning, middle, and end.	SA	A	D
Events are presented in chronological order.	SA	A	D
I painted a clear picture by using adjectives and adverbs effectively.	SA	A	D
I shared my feelings about what happened to me.	SA	A	D

Part C: On a scale of 1 to 10, assign a grade to your recount: _____

Explain why.

Pembroke Publishers ©2022 *Write to Read* by Larry Swartz ISBN 978-1-55138-359-0

Thinking Stems Sample Prompts

I know…

I predict…

I like…

I don't like…

I disagree with…

I connect with…

I learned…

I feel…

I hope…

I imagine…

I pictured/visualized…

I remember…

I am reminded of…

I want to know more about…

I am puzzled by…

I wonder…

Pembroke Publishers ©2022 *Write to Read* by Larry Swartz ISBN 978-1-55138-359-0

Tic-Tac-Toe Chart

an empty well 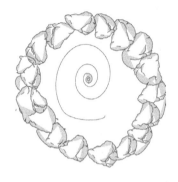	a dark forest 	a lost animal 
a magic mirror 	a jewelled crown 	a heavy suitcase 
a torn map 	a rusty key 	an ancient book 

Pembroke Publishers ©2022 *Write to Read* by Larry Swartz ISBN 978-1-55138-359-0

Zodiac Charts

The Constellation Zodiac

Aries: The Ram / March 21 to April 19
Taurus: The Bull / April 20 to May 19
Gemini: The Twins / May 20 to June 20
Cancer: The Crab/ June 21 to July 22
Leo: The Lion / July 23 to August 21
Virgo: The Maiden / August 22 to September 22
Libra: The Scales / September 22 to October 22
Scorpio: The Scorpion / October 23 to November 21
Sagittarius: The Archer / November 22 to December 21
Capricorn: The Goat / December 22 to January 20
Aquarius: The Water-Bearer / January 21 to February 19
Pisces: The Fish / February 20 to March 20

The Chinese Zodiac

2008	Feb. 7, 2008– Jan. 25, 2009	Year of the Rat
2009	Jan. 26, 2009 – Feb. 13, 2010	Year of the Ox
2010	Feb. 14, 2010 – Feb. 2, 2011	Year of the Tiger
2011	Feb. 3, 2011 – Jan. 22, 2012	Year of the Rabbit
2012	Jan. 23, 2012 – Feb. 9, 2013	Year of the Dragon
2013	Feb. 10, 2013 – Jan. 30, 2014	Year of the Snake
2014	Jan. 31, 2014 – Feb. 18, 2015	Year of the Horse
2015	Feb. 19, 2015 – Feb. 7, 2016	Year of the Goat
2016	Feb. 8, 2016 – Jan. 27, 2017	Year of the Monkey
2017	Jan. 28, 2017 – Feb. 15, 2018	Year of the Rooster
2018	Feb. 16, 2018 – Feb. 4, 2019	Year of the Dog
2019	Feb. 4, 2019 – Jan. 24, 2020	Year of the Pig

Pembroke Publishers ©2022 *Write to Read* by Larry Swartz ISBN 978-1-55138-359-0

Thinking About My Writing

Name _____

The following statements will help you think about your life as a writer.

PART A: Answer Strongly Agree (SA), Agree (A), Disagree (D), or Strongly Disagree (SD)

I enjoy writing.	SA	A	D	SD
I often write outside of school.	SA	A	D	SD
I like when the teacher assigns a prompt or topic for writing.	SA	A	D	SD
I often get ideas for writing from books.	SA	A	D	SD
It takes me a long time to think about what to write.	SA	A	D	SD
Getting feedback from a teacher or a classmate often helps me with my writing.	SA	A	D	SD
I like writing made-up stories more than factual stories.	SA	A	D	SD
I willingly spend time revising and editing my work.	SA	A	D	SD
Talking before writing is useful to me.	SA	A	D	SD
I often like sharing my writing with others.	SA	A	D	SD

PART B: Complete these statements…

My favorite piece(s) of writing are …

Something or things I might do to improve my writing:

A good writer is someone who…

How would you describe yourself as a writer?

Thought Starters

Tell…

1. What makes you happy. Or proud.
2. About a time you were frustrated or angry or afraid.
3. A story about travelling to the past or the future.
4. A story about going camping, or going to a sleepover, or going shopping.
5. About what happened in a dream you remember.
6. About an argument you had with someone. How did it get solved (or not)?
7. About your life as a pencil (or computer, or bicycle, or skateboard).
8. Everything someone needs to know about your friend (brother or sister, babysitter, parent).
9. What you would write to a bully in a letter.

Questions to Consider

10. Where would you prefer to visit: a museum, a gallery, a sports stadium? Why?
11. What is a problem in the world that you would like to help change?
12. What movie would you like to watch again and again and again?
13. What would you do if you won the lottery?
14. What was your day like yesterday?
15. How does your pet cheer you up?
16. What would you like to invent?
17. How would you describe yourself to someone who didn't know you?
18. How important is a computer (or phone or TV) in your life?
19. What is the hardest thing about being your age? The best thing?
20. Which story character would you like to talk to? What would you say/ask?
21. Which superpower would you like to have?
22. What do you like best about your family?
23. Which of the four seasons is your favorite?
24. What is your bedtime routine (or morning routine)?
25. Would you rather be friends with a unicorn or a space alien?

Complete the Statement

26. Today (or yesterday) started out like any other day, but then…
27. If I were an animal…
28. My most favorite book in the whole world is…
29. I would love to own a robot because…
30. My best birthday party was…
31. When I look out my window, I see…
32. I remember a day at the beach when…
33. A few of my favorite things are…
34. I remember the first time I…
35. I know a lot about…
36. I wonder…

Pembroke Publishers ©2022 *Write to Read* by Larry Swartz ISBN 978-1-55138-359-0

Revision Checklist

Content Checklist

- ☐ Did I say everything I wanted to say?
- ☐ Did I say it the way I wanted to say it?
- ☐ Did I say it clearly so that others will understand what I wrote?
- ☐ Did I include all necessary information?
- ☐ Should I leave out some ideas?
- ☐ Should I change some of my ideas?
- ☐ Did I present events, ideas, steps in a logical order?
- ☐ Did I write a good beginning, middle, and end?
- ☐ Did I vary my sentence types?
- ☐ When I used paragraphs, did all sentences belong with the topic sentence of the paragraph?
- ☐ Did I use the most accurate and interesting words I could think of?

Proofreading Checklist

- ☐ Does each sentence make sense?
- ☐ Does the order of words in each sentence make sense?
- ☐ Is my grammar correct?
- ☐ Have I punctuated each sentence correctly?
- ☐ Have I used capital letters correctly?
- ☐ When I used direct speech, did I punctuate it correctly?
- ☐ Did I spell words correctly, checking words about which I was unsure?
- ☐ Did I use proper form for titles, indenting, margins?

The Writing Process

- ☐ Did I prepare a draft or drafts and revise work to publication?
- ☐ Did I comply with instructions for each writing task?
- ☐ Did I use examples from literature to support my writing?
- ☐ Did I get (and use) feedback from others?
- ☐ Did I willingly revise and edit the work?
- ☐ Did I successfully meet the success criteria for each genre?

Pembroke Publishers ©2022 *Write to Read* by Larry Swartz ISBN 978-1-55138-359-0

Assessment Checklist

Student Name: _____   Date: _____

Consistently
Often
Sometimes
Not **Y**et

Student demonstrates ability to	C	O	S	NY
generate writing that is clear and engages the reader				
organize and present ideas in logical sequence and paragraphs				
support ideas with details and feelings				
vary sentences and use dialogue effectively				
include style techniques such titles, lead sentences, voice, text features				
choose vivid vocabulary to bring meaning to the text				
write complete sentences with few errors				
edit for spelling, punctuation, and revision of sentences				
revise and improve work after receiving feedback				
use success criteria to meet expectations for each writing project				
develop writing from draft to publication that engages readers				
enjoy writing and be self-motivated				

Writing Goal

Dr. Larry Recommends

Mentor Books for Writing

Alphabet Books

ABC x 3: English, Español, Français by Marthe Jocelyn; illus. Tom Slaughter

A is for Activist by Innosanto Nagara

A is for Bee: An alphabet book in translation by Ellen Heck

A to Z by Sandra Boynton

Alphabeasties: and other AmaZing types by Sharon Werner and Sarah Forss

Chicka Chicka Boom Boom by Bill Martin Jr. and John Archambault; illus. Lois Ehlert

Bad Kitty by Nick Bruel

Eating the Alphabet: Fruits and Vegetables from A to Z by Lois Ehlert

The Hidden Alphabet by Laura Vaccaro Seeger

Inclusion Alphabet: ABC's for Everyone by Kathryn Jenkins

A Northern Alphabet by Ted Harrison

Olivia's ABC by Ian Falconer

Once Upon an Alphabet by Oliver Jeffers

P is for Pterodactyl by Raj Halder and Chris Carpenter; illus. Maria Tina Beddia

West Coast Wild by Deborah Hodge; illus. Karen Reczuch

Biographies

Every Day is Malala Day by Rosemary McCarney

Freedom Over Me: Eleven slaves, their lives and dreams brought to life by Ashley Bryan

I Am Not a Label: 34 Disabled Artists, Thinkers, Athletes and Activists from Past and Present by Cerrie Burnell; illus. Lauren Baldo

The Important Thing about Margaret Wise Brown by Mac Barnett; illus. Sarah Jacoby

Martin's Big Words by Doreen Rappaport; illus. Bryan Collier

Nelson Mandela by Kadir Nelson

A Poem for Peter: The Story of Ezra Jack Keats and the creation of The Snowy Day by Andrea Davis Pinkney; illus. Louise Fancher and Steve Johnson

Radiant Child: The story of Young Artist Jean-Michel Basquiat by Javaka Steptoe

Rosa by Nikki Giovanni; illus. Bryan Collier

Six Dots: A story of young Louis Braille by Jen Bryant; illus. Boris Kulikov

Some Writer! The story of E.B. White by Melissa Sweet

Unstoppable: Women with Disabilities by Helen Wolfe; illus. Karen Patkau

Viola Desmond Won't Be Budged! by Jody Nyasha Warner; illus. Richard Rudnicki

Dialogue

Duck! Rabbit! by Amy Krouse Rosenthal; illus. Tom Lichtenheld

I Want My Hat Back by Jon Klassen

It's a Book! by Lane Smith

No, David (series) by David Shannon

Yo! Yes? by Chris Raschka (also *Ring! Yo?*)

Diaries

Picture Books

Amelia's Notebook by Marissa Moss (series)

Diary of a Worm by Doreen Cronin; illus. Harry Bliss (also *Diary of a Fly; Diary of a Spider*)

Diary of a Wombat by Jackie French; illus. Bruce Whatley

Max's Logbook by Marissa Moss

Fiction Series

Diary of a Minecraft Zombie by Zack Zombie

Diary of a Wimpy Kid by Jeff Kinney

Dork Diaries by Rachel Renée Russell

The Mutts Diaries (series) by Patrick McDonnell

The Tom Gates Diaries by Liz Pichon

Owl Diaries by Rebecca Elliott (also: Unicorn Diaries)

The Princess Diaries by Meg Cabot

Free Verse Novels

Brown Girl Dreaming by Jacqueline Woodson

The Crazy Man by Pamela Porter

Ebb and Flow by Heather Smith

The Gospel Truth by Caroline Pignat

Home of the Brave by Katherine Applegate

Inside Out and Back Again by Thanhhà Lai

Love that Dog by Sharon Creech (also *Hate That Cat; Moo*)

One by Sarah Crossan
Out of the Dust by Karen Hesse

Graphic Texts

Babymouse (series) by Jennifer Holm; illus. Matthew Holm
Bone (series) by Jeff Smith
Borders by Thomas King; illus. Natasha Donovan
Dog Man (series) by Dav Pilkey (also Captain Underpants series; Cat Kid Comic Club series)
Dragon Hoops by Gene Luen Yang
El Deafo by Cece Bell
The Good Fight by Ted Staunton; illus. Josh Rosen
Guts by Raina Telgemeier (also *Smile*; *Drama*)
Long Way Down: The Graphic Novel by Jason Reynolds; illus. Danica Novgorodoff (YA)
New Kid by Jerry Craft (sequel: *Class Act*)
Real Friends by Shannon Hale; illus. LeUyen Pham (sequels: *Best Friends, Friends Forever*)
When Stars Are Scattered by Victoria Jamieson and Omar Mohamed

How-To/Procedurals

Be You! by Peter H. Reynolds
Everyone Can Learn to Ride a Bicycle by Chris Raschka
How to Babysit a Grandpa by Jean Reagan; illus. Lee Wildish (also: *How To Babysit a Grandma*)
How to Make an Apple Pie and See the World by Marjorie Priceman
How to Read a Book by Kwame Alexander; illus. Melissa Sweet
So You Want to Talk about Race by Ijeoma Oluo
What Can I Say? A kids guide to super-useful social skills to help you get along and express yourself by Catherine Newman; illus. Debbie Fong (also: *How To Be a Person*)

Journals

All About Me: a guided journal all about the awesomeness of me from C. R. Gibson
All About Me: A keepsake journal for kids by Linda Kranz
A Day in the Life of Me: Kids Daily Journal and Healthy Habit Tracker by June and Lucy Kids
Dork Diaries: OMG! All About Me Diary! by Rachel Renée Russell
Find Your Voice: A guided journal for writing your truth by Angie Thomas
My Notebook (with help from Amelia) by Marissa Moss
This Book is Anti-Racist Journal by Tiffany Jewell; ills, Aurelia Durand

Letters

Picture Books

Click, Clack, Moo: Cows That Type by Doreen Cronin; illus. Betsy Lewin
Can I Be Your Dog? by Troy Cummings
The Day the Crayons Quit by Drew Daywalt; illus. Oliver Jeffers
Dear Dragon: A Pen Pal Tale by Josh Funk; illus. Rodolfo Montalvo
Dear Mr. Blueberry by Simon James
Dear Mrs. LaRue: Letters from Obedience School (series) by Mark Teague
Dear Teacher by Amy Husband
I Wanna Iguana by Karen Kaufman Orloff; illus. David Catrow (also: *I Wanna New Room*)
The Gardener by Sarah Stewart; illus. David Small
The Jolly Postman by Janet and Allan Ahlberg
Letters from Space by Clayton Anderson; illus. Susan Batori
Please Write Soon: The Unforgettable Story of Two Cousins in World War II by Michael Rosen; illus. Michael Foreman
Ten Thank You Letters by Daniel Kirk
Yours Truly, Goldilocks by Alma Flor Ada; illus. Leslie Tryon (also *Dear Peter Rabbit*)

Fiction

Dear Hank Williams by Kimberly Willis Holt
Dear Mr. Henshaw by Beverly Cleary
Dear Martin by Nic Stone (YA)
Letters from Cuba by Ruth Behar
Letters from Rifka by Karen Hesse
The Night Diary by Veera Hiranandani
The Perks of Being a Wallflower by Stephen Chbosky (YA)

Lists

Goodnight Moon by Margaret Wise Brown; illus. Clement Hurd
I Am Every Good Thing by Derrick Barnes; illus. Gordon C. James
Just Because by Mac Barnett; illus. Isabelle Arsenault
The Important Book by Margaret Wise Brown; illus. Leonard Weisgard
Miss Bindergarten Gets Ready for Kindergarten by Joseph Slate; illus. Ashley Wolff

News Reports

Amy Namey in Ace Reporter by Megan McDonald; Illus. Erwin Madrid (chapter book)

The Breaking News by Sarah Lynne Reul

I Can Write the World by Joshunda Sanders; illus. Charly Palmer

The Nantucket Sea Monster: A fake news story by Darcy Pattison; illus. Peter Willis

On the News: Our first talk about tragedy by Dr Jillian Roberts; illus. Jane Heinrichs (nonfiction)

Observations

Honeybee: The Busy Life of Apis Mellifera by Candace Fleming; illus. Eric Rohmann

Bat Citizens: Defending the Ninjas of the Night by Rob Laidlaw

How to Be an Elephant by Katherine Roy

Loon by Susan Vande Griek; illus. Karen Reczuch

Martin and the River by Jon-Erik Lappano; illus. Josée Bisaillon

Outside, You Notice by Erin Alladin; illus. Andrea Blinick

An Owl at Sea by Susan Vande Griek, illus. Ian Wallace

Turtle Pond by James Gladstone; illus. Karen Reczuch

Patterns

The Best Part of Me by Wendy Ewald

Brown Bear, Brown Bear, What do you see? (series) by Bill Martin Jr; illus. Eric Carle

The Day the Crayons Quit by Drew Daywalt; illus. Oliver Jeffers

I Am Every Good Thing by Derrick C. Barnes; illus. Gordon C. James

The Important Book by Margaret Wise Brown; illus. Leonard Weisgard

Reading Makes You Feel Good by Todd Parr (also *The Kindness Book*; *The Peace Book*; *The Thankful* Book)

Sometimes I Feel Like a Fox by Danielle Daniel

Somewhere Today by Shelley Moore Thomas; Photography Eric Fultran

This Is a School by John Schu; illus. Veronical Miller Jamison

What Does Peace Feel Like? By Vladimir Radunsky

Would You Rather...? by John Burningham

Persuasion

Click, Clack, Moo! Cows That Type by Doreen Cronin; illus. Betsy Lewin

The Day the Crayons Quit by Drew Daywalt; illus. Oliver Jeffers

Dear Mr. President by Sophie Siers; illus. Anne Villeneuve

Don't Let the Pigeon Drive the Bus by Mo Willems

Have I Got a Book for You! by Mélanie Watt

I Wanna Iguana by Karen Kaufman Orloff; ills David Catrow (also: *I Wanna New Room*)

Hey, Little Ant by Phillip and Hannah Hoose; illus. by Debbie Tilley

Red Is Best by Kathy Stinson; illus. Robin Baird Lewis

Poetry

The Bully, The Bullied, The Bystander, The Brave by David Booth and Larry Swartz (eds.)

The Dream Keeper and other poems by Langston Hughes

Everything Comes Next by Naomi Shihab Nye

Guyku: A Year of Haiku for Boys by Bob Raczka; illus. Peter H. Reynolds

Hawks Kettle, Puffins Wheel and Other Poems of Birds in Flight by Susan Vande Griek; illus. Mark Hoffmann

Head to Toe Spaghetti and other tasty poems by David Booth; illus. Les Drew (also: *Bird Guy*)

Our Corner Store by Robert Heidbreder; illus. Chelsea O'Byrne (also: *Rooster Summer*)

Out of Wonder: Poems celebrating poets edited by Kwame Alexander, Chris Colderley, and Marjory Wentworth; illus. Ekua Holmes

Say Her Name by Zetta Elliott; illus. Loveis Wise

Summer Feet by Sheree Fitch; illus. Carolyn Fisher

The Place My Words are Looking For edited by Paul B. Janeczko (ed.)

Tiger, Tiger Burning Bright! An animal poem for each day of the year edited by Fiona Waters ; illus. Britta Teckentrup

'Til All the Stars Have Fallen edited by David Booth; illus. Kady MacDonald Denton

Whoo-ku Haiku: A great horned owl story by Maria Gianferrari; illus. Jonathan Voss

Questions

Ada Twist, Scientist by Andrea Beaty; illus. David Roberts

Ask Me by Bernard Waber; illus. Suzy Lee

Avocado Asks by Momoko Abe

The Boy, The Mole, The Fox and the Horse by Charlie Mackesy

A Chicken Followed Me Home! by Robin Page

If... by Sarah Perry

If You Were Night by Muon Thi Van; illus. Kelly Pousette

Just Ask by Sonia Sotomayor; illus. Rafael López

Just Because by Mac Barnett; illus. Isabelle Arsenault

Mama, Do You Love Me? Barbara M Joosse; illus. Barbara Lavallee

The Three Questions by Jon J. Muth

Why? The best ever question and answer book about nature, science and the world around you by Catherine Ripley; illus. Scot Ritchie

Recounts

Alexander and the Terrible, Horrible, No Good Very Bad Day by Judith Viorst; illus. Ray Cruz

The Doll by Nhung N. Tran-Davies; illus. Ravy Puth

Fireflies! by Julie Brinckloe

The Relatives Came by Cynthia Rylant; illus. Stephen Gammell

Grandfather's Journey by Allen Say

Jabari Jumps by Gaia Cornwall (also: *Jabari Tries*)

Last Stop on Market Street by Matt de la Peña; illus. Christian Robinson

New Shoes by Chris Raschka

Owl Moon by Jane Yolen; illus. John Schoenherr

Word Power

Big Words for Little Geniuses by Susan and James Patterson; illus. Hsinping Pan (also: *Bigger Words for Little Geniuses*)

Cassie's Word Quilt by Faith Ringgold

Donovan's Word Jar by Monalisa de Gross

Fancy Nancy (series) by Jane O'Connor; illus. Robin Preiss Glasser

Maisy's Amazing Big Book of Words by Lucy Cousins

Max's Words by Kate Banks; illus. Boris Kulikov

Richard Scarry's Best Word Book Ever by Richard Scarry

Today by Julie Morstad

The Word Collector by Peter H. Reynolds

Worser by Jennifer Ziegler (novel)

Professional Resources

Alexander, Kwame (2019). *The Write Thing.* Huntington Beach, CA: Shell Education.

Booth, David (2016). *Literacy 101.* Markham, ON: Pembroke.

Booth, David and Bob Barton (2004). *Poetry Goes to School.* Markham, ON: Pembroke.

Booth, David and Larry Swartz (2004). *Literacy Techniques, 2nd Edition.* Markham, ON: Pembroke.

Buis, Kellie (2007). *Reclaiming Reluctant Writers.* Markham, ON: Pembroke

Donohue, Lisa (2009). *The Write Beginning.* Markham, ON: Pembroke.

_____ (2011). *The Write Voice.* Markham, ON: Pembroke.

Dorfman, Lynne R. and Rose Cappelli (2009). *Nonfiction Mentor Texts.* Portland, ME: Stenhouse.

_____ (2017). *Mentor Texts, 2nd edition.* Portland, ME: Stenhouse.

Filewych, Karen (2017). *How Do I Get Them To Write?* Markham, ON. Pembroke

_____ (2019). *Freewriting with Purpose.* Markham, ON: Pembroke.

Fletcher, Ralph (2015). *Making Nonfiction from Scratch.* Portland, ME: Stenhouse.

Fletcher, Ralph and JoAnn Portalupi (2007). *Craft Lessons, 2nd edition.* Portland, ME: Stenhouse.

_____ (2001). *Nonfiction Craft Lessons.* Portland, ME: Stenhouse.

Gear, Adrienne (2011). *Writing Power.* Markham, ON: Pembroke.

_____ (2014). *Nonfiction Writing Power.* Markham, ON: Pembroke.

_____ (2020). *Powerful Writing Structures.* Markham, ON: Pembroke.

_____ (2021). *Powerful Poetry.* Markham, ON: Pembroke.

Harwayne, Shelley (2021). *Above and Beyond the Writing Workshop.* Portland, ME: Stenhouse.

Miller, Donalyn (2009). *The Book Whisperer: Awakening the Inner Reader in Every Child.* San Francisco, CA: Jossey-Boss.

Miller, Donalyn and Susan Kelley (2013). *Reading in the Wild: The Book Whisperer's Keys to Cultivating Lifelong Reading Habits.* San Francisco, CA: Jossey-Boss.

Paul, Pamela and Maria Russo (2019). *How to Raise a Reader.* New York, NY: Workman.

Pennac, Daniel (1999). *Better Than Life.* Markham, ON: Pembroke.

Peterson, Shelley Stagg (2005). *Writing Across the Curriculum: All teachers teach writing.* Winnipeg, MB: Portage & Main Press.

Peterson, Shelley Stagg, and Larry Swartz (2015). *This is a Great Book!* Markham, ON: Pembroke.

Rog, Lori Jamison and Paul Kropp (2004). *The Write Genre.* Markham, ON: Pembroke.

Routman, Regie (2018). *Literacy Essentials: Engagement, Excellence, and Equity for All Learners.* Portland, ME: Stenhouse.

Swartz, Larry. (2017). *Take Me to Your Readers.* Markham, ON: Pembroke.

_____ (2019). *Word by Word.* Markham, ON: Pembroke.

_____ (2020). *Teaching Tough Topics.* Markham, ON: Pembroke.

_____ (2020). "Choosing and Using Nonfiction Picture Books in the Classroom" in Grilli, Giorgia (ed.) *Non-Fiction Picture Books: Sharing Knowledge as an Aesthetic Experience.* Pisa, IT: Edizioni ETS

_____ (2021). *Better Reading Now.* Markham, ON: Pembroke

Swartz, Larry, Debbie Nyman, and Magdalin Livingston (2021). *Deepening In-Class and Online Learning.* Markham ON: Pembroke.

Swartz, Larry and Sheree Fitch (2008). *The Poetry Experience.* Markham, ON: Pembroke.

Swope, Sam (2005). *I Am a Pencil: A Teacher, His Kids, and Their World of Stories.* New York, NY: Henry Holt and Company.

Wilhelm, Jeffrey D., Peggy Jo Wilhelm, and Erika Boas (2009). *Inquiring Minds Learn to Read and Write: 50 Problem-Based Literacy and Learning Strategies.* Oakville, ON: Rubicon.

Index